Glencoe

Algebra 1

Integration
Applications
Connections

Modeling Mathematics
Masters

GLENCOE

McGraw-Hill

New York, New York   Columbus, Ohio   Woodland Hills, California   Peoria, Illinois

Glencoe/McGraw-Hill

A Division of The **McGraw·Hill** *Companies*

Send all inquiries to:
Glencoe/McGraw-Hill
936 Eastwind Drive
Westerville, OH 43081-3329

Algebra I
Modeling Mathematics Masters

ISBN: 0-02-824848-1

4 5 6 7 8 9 10 066 03 02 01 00 99 98

Contents

Overview

This booklet contains a variety of materials that can help students learn the concepts and skills of algebra. These materials are divided into four sections: Easy-to-Make Manipulatives, Modeling Mathematics Worksheets, Modeling Mathematics Activities, and Cooperative Learning Activities.

Easy-to-Make Manipulatives can be used throughout the course to support the development of key concepts using visual and concrete materials.

Modeling Mathematics Worksheets correspond to Modeling Mathematics lessons in the Student Edition. Some worksheets serve as recording sheets for students to use as they complete Modeling Mathematics lessons. Other worksheets provide additional exercises similar to those in the Modeling Mathematics lessons.

Modeling Mathematics Activities focus on fundamental concepts and skills that are necessary for success in algebra. These activities can be used to introduce a lesson or to reinforce or review the objectives of a lesson. There is one page of teaching suggestions for each activity, as well as a Transparency Master and a student worksheet. The Transparency Masters are to be used to make transparencies for use with an overhead projector or to make copies for direct student use. Answers to the problems on each student worksheet appear on the back of the worksheet.

Cooperative Learning Activities offer many valuable opportunities for students to analyze, form hypotheses, and reach conclusions using a group approach. It is recommended that groups be allowed to devise their own approach to dividing work and combining results. The activities can benefit from group discussion and brainstorming in the early stages of analyzing a problem. Strive for full participation by all group members and encourage students to present organized oral or written reports that summarize problem-solving approaches and results.

Although each activity master is recommended for use after a particular lesson, your judgment and sensitivity to the special needs of your students may convince you to modify our recommendations. Please feel free to do so.

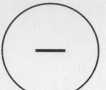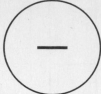

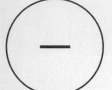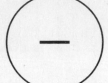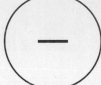

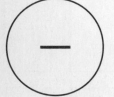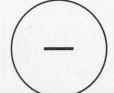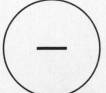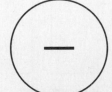

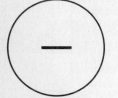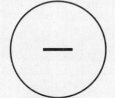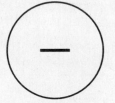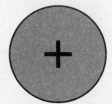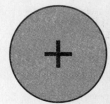

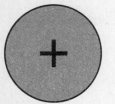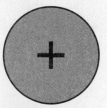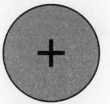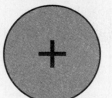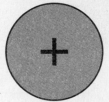

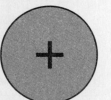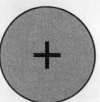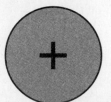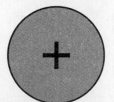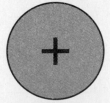

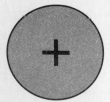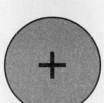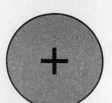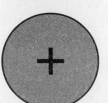

Algebra 1

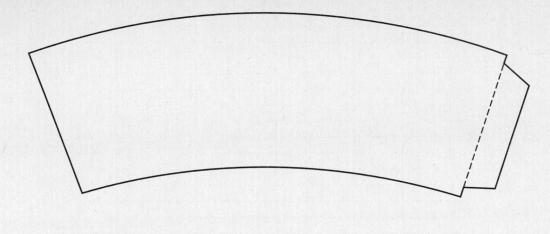

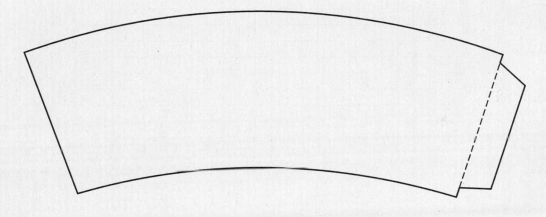

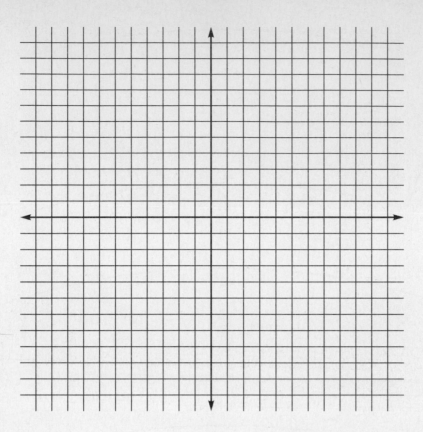

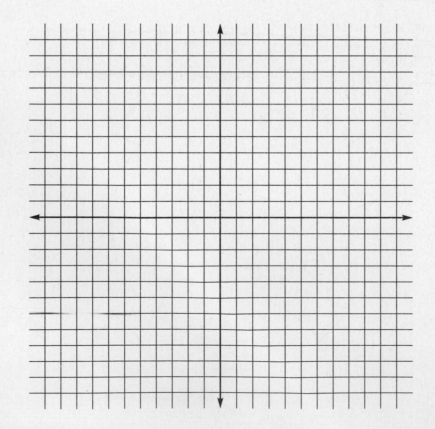

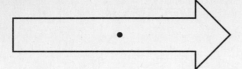

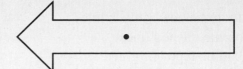

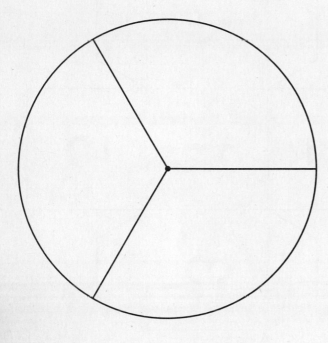

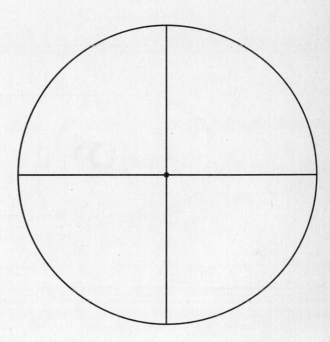

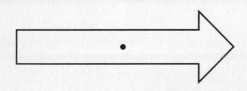

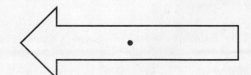

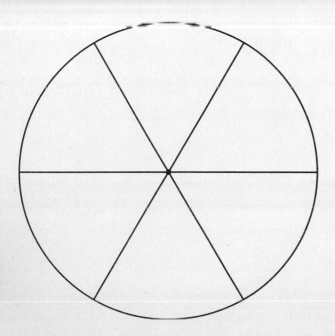

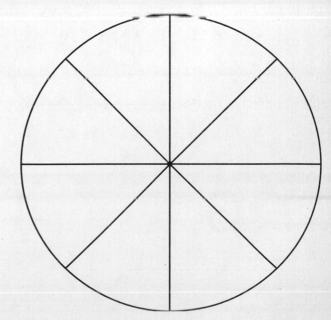

Cut along the heavy black lines.
Fold on the dashed lines.
Tabs can be taped or glued.

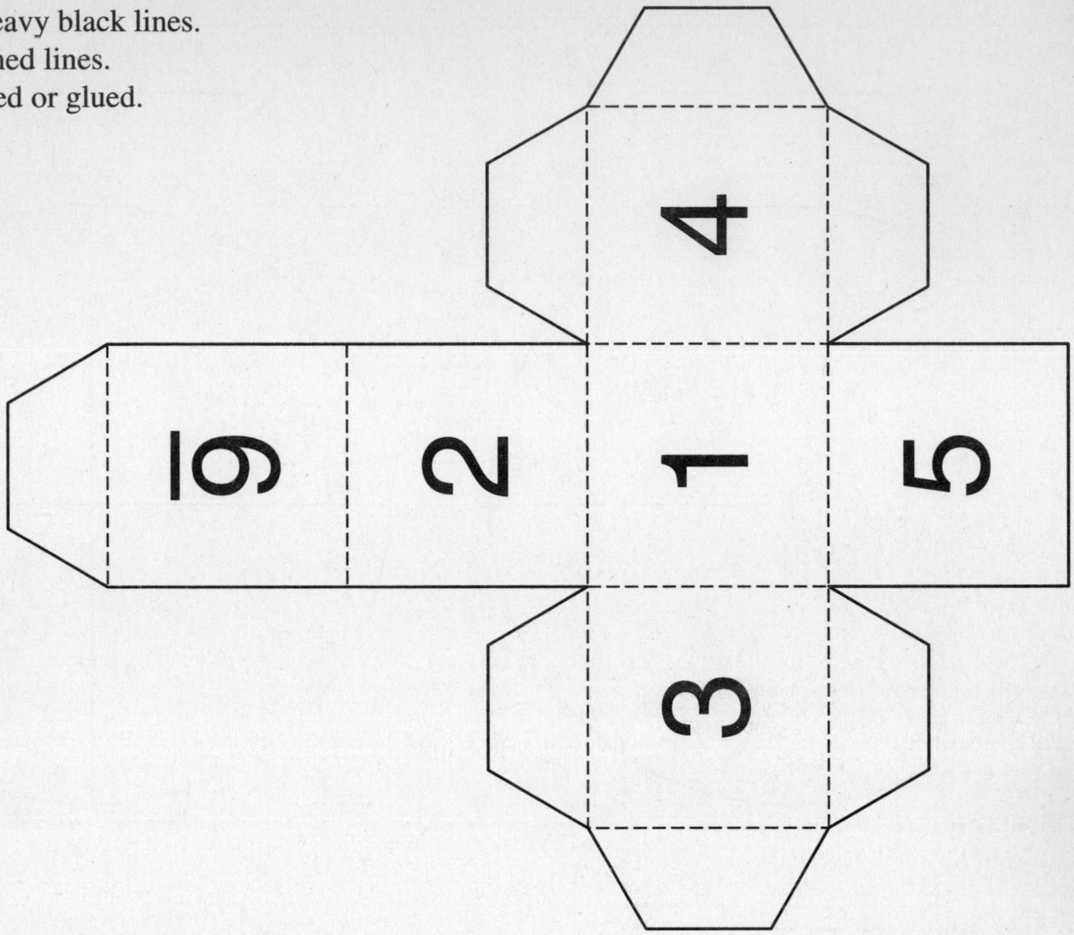

4

6   2   1   5

3

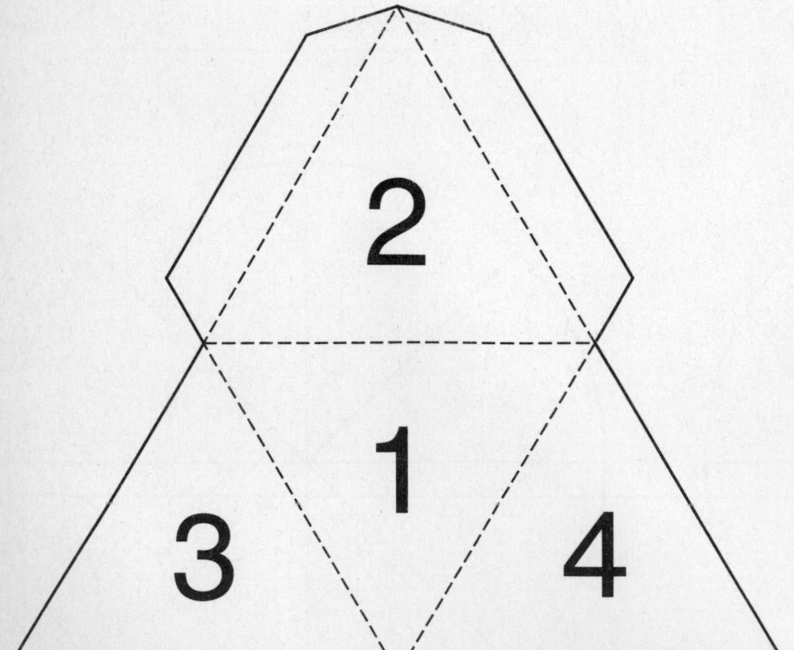

2

3   1   4

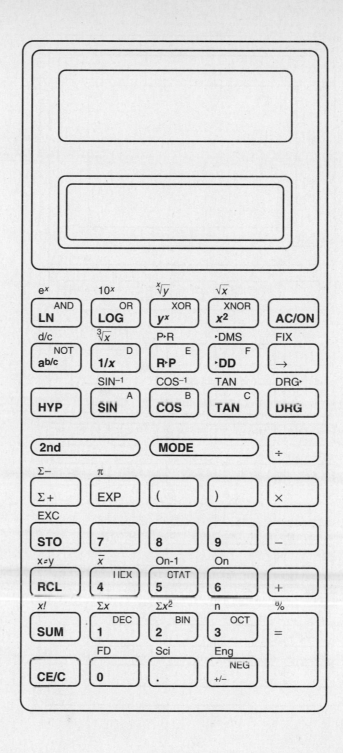

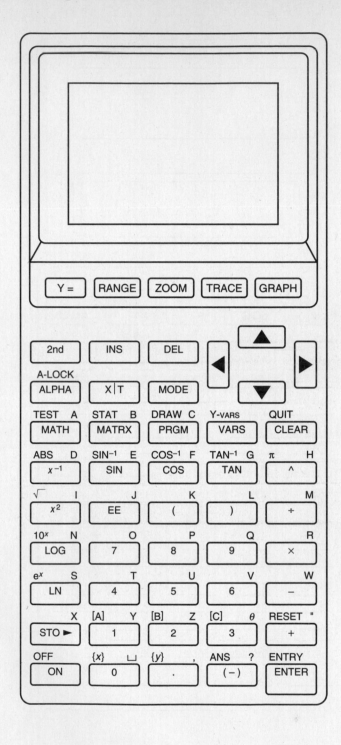

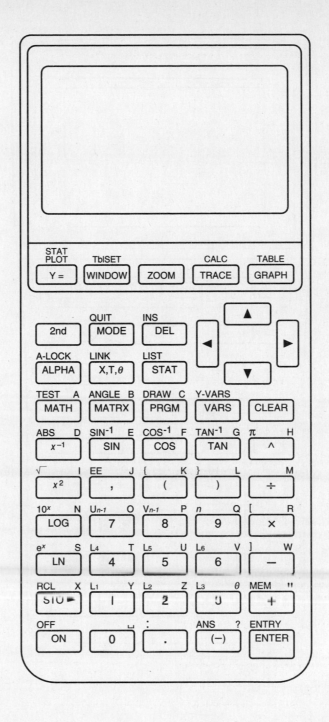

Calculator Layout
(Casio fx-7700 GE)

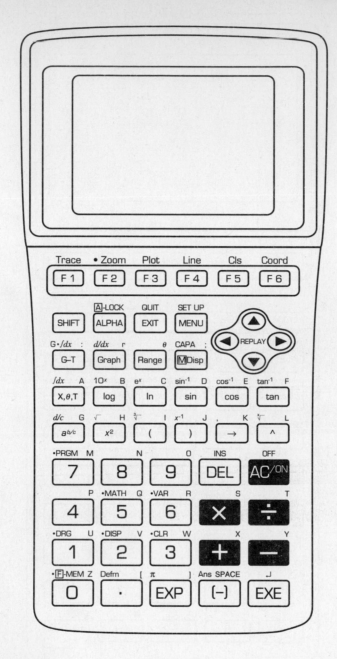

$$=$$

Product Mats

15

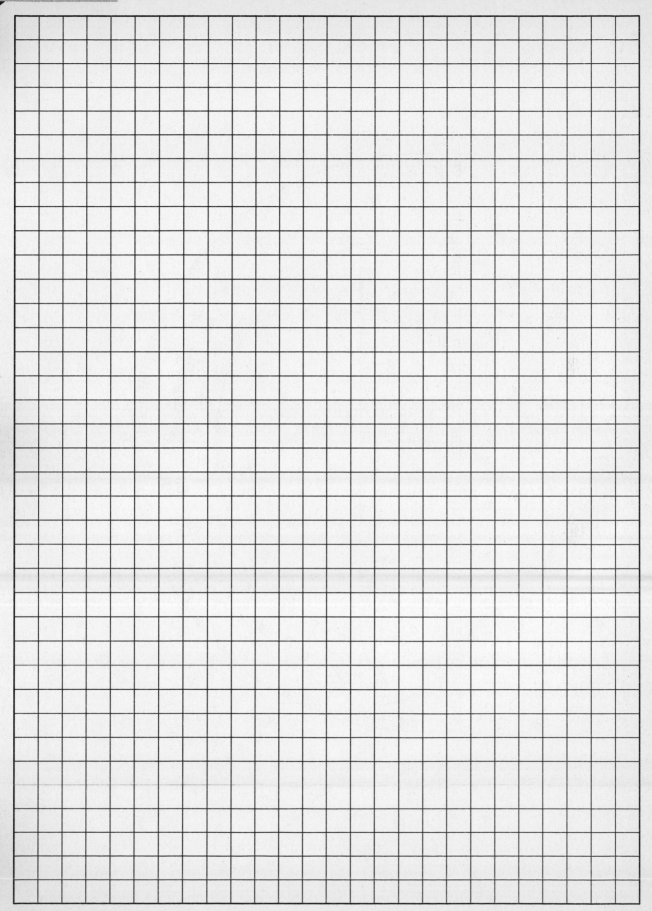

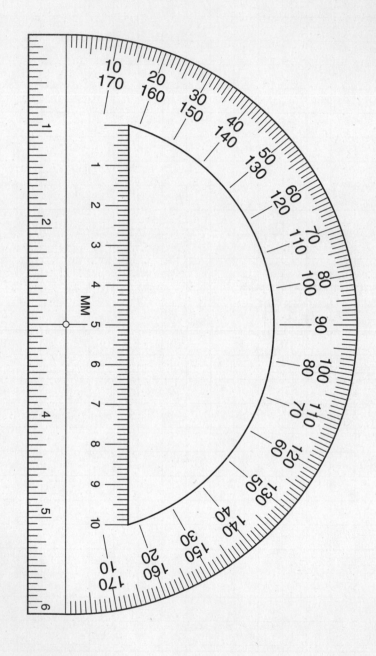

Modeling Mathematics

The Distributive Property

Algebra tiles and a product mat can be used to model a product as the area of a rectangle. In the figure below, algebra tiles have been arranged on a product mat to model the product $3(2x + 2)$.

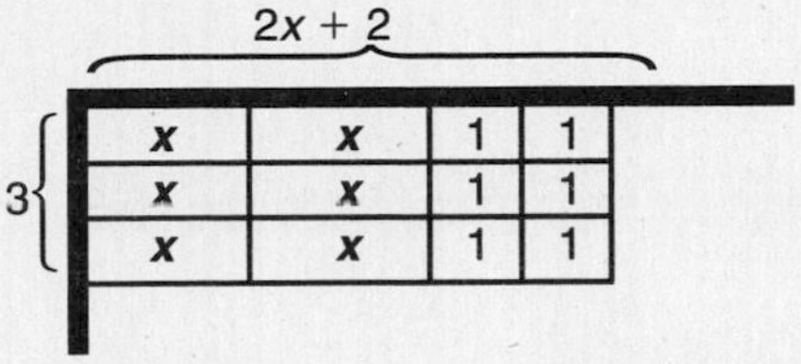

The rectangle has a width of 3 units and a length of $x + 2$ units. The rectangle has 6 x-tiles and 6 1-tiles. The area of the rectangle can be expressed $6x + 6$. So, $3(2x + 2) = 6x + 6$.

Fill in the blanks to describe what each arrangement of algebra tiles represents.

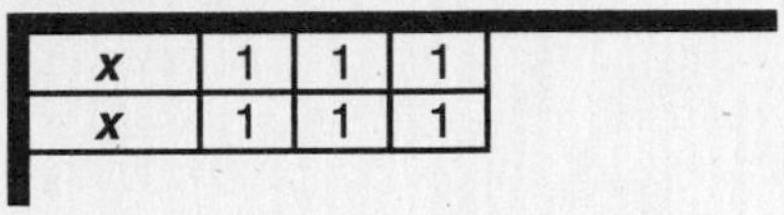

1. _____ = _____

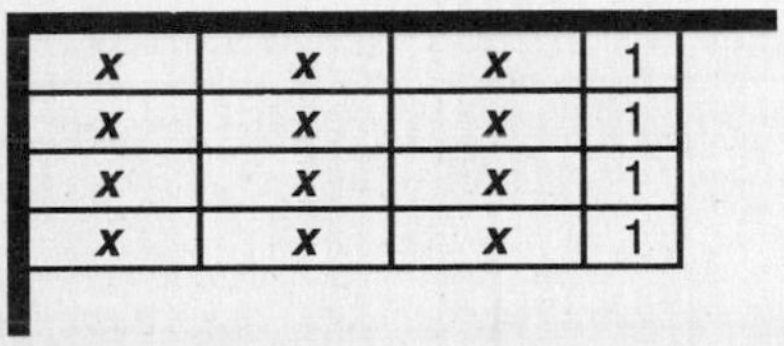

2. _____ = _____

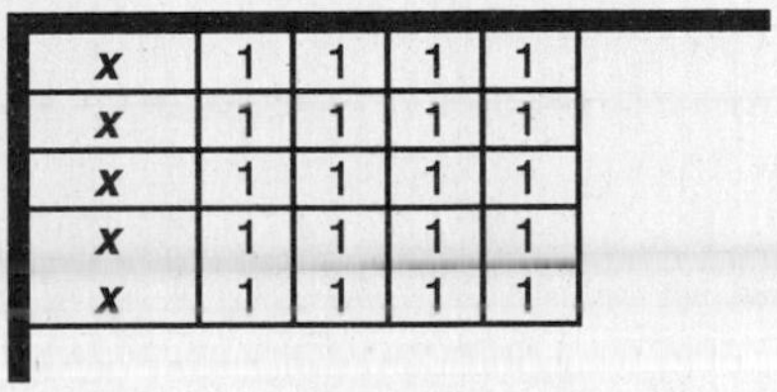

3. _____ = _____

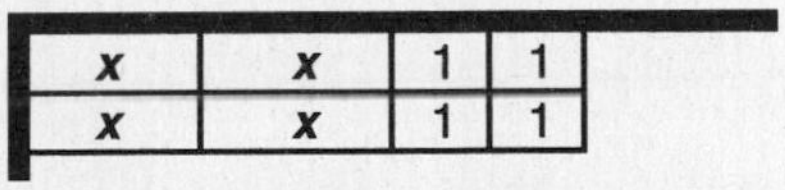

4. _____ = _____

Use algebra tiles to model each product. Then draw a picture of the model.

5. $4(x + 1)$

6. $2(3x + 2)$

Modeling Mathematics

The Distributive Property

Algebra tiles and a product mat can be used to model a product as the area of a rectangle. In the figure below, algebra tiles have been arranged on a product mat to model the product $3(2x + 2)$.

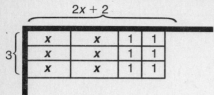

2x + 2

3

x	x	1	1
x	x	1	1
x	x	1	1

The rectangle has a width of 3 units and a length of $x + 2$ units. The rectangle has 6 x-tiles and 6 1-tiles. The area of the rectangle can be expressed $6x + 6$. So, $3(2x + 2) = 6x + 6$.

Fill in the blanks to describe what each arrangement of algebra tiles represents.

| x | 1 | 1 | 1 |
| x | 1 | 1 | 1 |

1. _____ = _____ $2(2x + 3) = 4x + 6$

x	x	x	1
x	x	x	1
x	x	x	1
x	x	x	1

2. _____ = _____ $4(3x + 1) = 12x + 4$

x	1	1	1	1
x	1	1	1	1
x	1	1	1	1
x	1	1	1	1
x	1	1	1	1

3. _____ = _____ $5(x + 4) = 5x + 20$

| x | x | 1 | 1 |
| x | x | 1 | 1 |

4. _____ = _____ $2(2x + 2) = 4x + 4$

Use algebra tiles to model each product. Then draw a picture of the model.

5. $4(x + 1)$

x	1
x	1
x	1
x	1

6. $2(3x + 2)$

| x | x | x | 1 | 1 |
| x | x | x | 1 | 1 |

NAME_____ DATE _____

Modeling Mathematics

Adding and Subtracting Integers

Find each sum or difference by using counters.

1. $4 + 2$

2. $4 + (-2)$

3. $-4 + 2$

_____   _____   _____

4. $-4 + (-2)$

5. $4 - 2$

6. $-4 - (-2)$

_____   _____   _____

7. $4 - (-2)$

8. $-4 - 2$

9. $1 - 4$

_____   _____   _____

10. $2 - (-7)$

11. $-3 + 6$

12. $-3 + 3$

_____   _____   _____

Tell whether each statement is true or false. Justify your answer with a drawing.

13. $5 - (-2) = 3$

14. $-5 + 7 = 2$

15. $2 - 3 = -1$

16. $-1 - 1 = 0$

 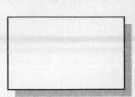

17. Write a paragraph explaining how to find the sum of two integers without using counters. Be sure to include all possibilities.

_____

_____

_____

_____

           Algebra 1

NAME_____ DATE _____

Modeling Mathematics

Adding and Subtracting Integers

Find each sum or difference by using counters.

1. $4 + 2$
    6

2. $4 + (-2)$
    2

3. $-4 + 2$
    −2

4. $-4 + (-2)$
    −6

5. $4 - 2$
    2

6. $-4 - (-2)$
    −2

7. $4 - (-2)$
    6

8. $-4 - 2$
    −6

9. $1 - 4$
    −3

10. $2 - (-7)$
    9

11. $-3 + 6$
    3

12. $-3 + 3$
    0

Tell whether each statement is true or false. Justify your answer with a drawing. **See students' drawings.**

13. $5 - (-2) = 3$

 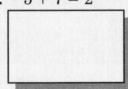

false

14. $-5 + 7 = 2$

 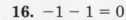

true

15. $2 - 3 = -1$

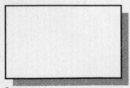 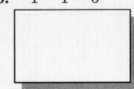

true

16. $-1 - 1 = 0$

false

17. Write a paragraph explaining how to find the sum of two integers without using counters. Be sure to include all possibilities.

Answers will vary. They should include using the number line for adding two negative integers, one negative and one positive integer, and two positive integers.

 Algebra 1

NAME_____ DATE _____

Modeling Mathematics

Multiplying Integers

1. What does $-2(-4)$ mean? Model this operation. Write your explanation in paragraph form.

_____

_____

_____

_____

Use counters to find each product.

2. $2(-5)$

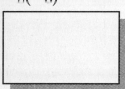

3. $-2(5)$

4. $-2(-5)$

5. $5(-2)$

6. $-5(2)$

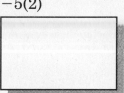

7. $-5(-2)$

8. How are the operations $-2(5)$ and $5(-2)$ the same? How do they differ?

_____

_____

21

Modeling Mathematics

Multiplying Integers

1. What does $-2(-4)$ mean? Model this operation. Write your explanation in paragraph form.

   See students' work.

   _____

   _____

   _____

Use counters to find each product. **See students' drawings.**

2. $2(-5)$

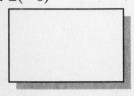

−10

3. $-2(5)$

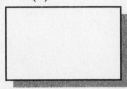

−10

4. $-2(-5)$

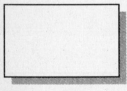

10

5. $5(-2)$

−10

6. $-5(2)$

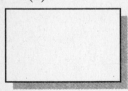

−10

7. $-5(-2)$

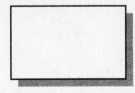

10

8. How are the operations $-2(5)$ and $5(-2)$ the same? How do they differ?

   The product is the same. The order of multiplication

   using counters is different.

NAME _____ DATE _____

Modeling Mathematics

Estimating Square Roots

Materials: base-ten tiles

You can use base-ten tiles to estimate the square root of a number.

To estimate the square root of 200, follow these steps.

Step 1: Use base-ten tiles to model the number 200.

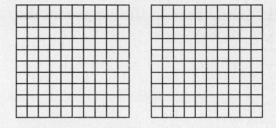

Step 2: Arrange the tiles into a square. Trade a 100-tile for ten 10-tiles and trade 10-tiles for 1-tiles as necessary. The largest square you can make has 196 tiles, with four 1-tiles left over.

Step 3: Add tiles until you have the next larger square. You need to add 25 tiles. Since 200 is between 196 (14^2) and 225 (15^2), the square root is between 14 and 15.

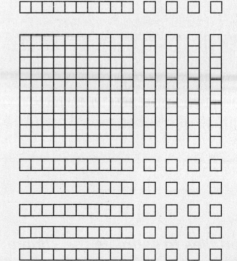

Use base-ten tiles to estimate the square root of each number.

1. 38 _____   2. 90 _____

3. 160 _____   4. 240 _____

NAME _____ DATE _____

Modeling Mathematics

Estimating Square Roots

Materials: base-ten tiles

You can use base-ten tiles to estimate the square root of a number.

To estimate the square root of 200, follow these steps.

Step 1: Use base-ten tiles to model the number 200.

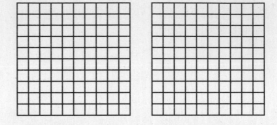

Step 2: Arrange the tiles into a square. Trade a 100-tile for ten 10-tiles and trade 10-tiles for 1-tiles as necessary. The largest square you can make has 196 tiles, with four 1-tiles left over.

Step 3: Add tiles until you have the next larger square. You need to add 25 tiles. Since 200 is between 196 (14^2) and 225 (15^2), the square root is between 14 and 15.

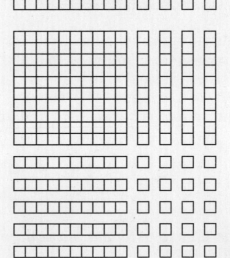

Use base-ten tiles to estimate the square root of each number.

1. 38 **6–7**

2. 90 **9–10**

3. 160 **12–13**

4. 240 **15–16**

3-1A

Modeling Mathematics

Solving One-Step Equations

Equation mats, cups, and counters can be used to model equations. The cups are used to represent an unknown number of positive or negative counters. Study the diagrams below.

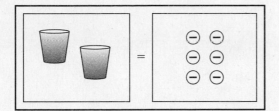
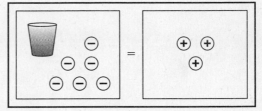

On the left side of the mat, the two cups represent two unknown values or $2x$. The right side of the mat has six negative counters representing -6. The equation represented on this mat is $2x = -6$.

On the left side of the mat, the cup represents an unknown value x and the six negative counters represent -6. Therefore, the left side of the mat represents $x + (-6)$. The three positive counters on the right side of the mat represent 3. The equation represented on this mat is $x + (-6) = 3$.

Write an equation for each equation mat.

1.
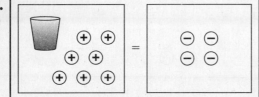

2.
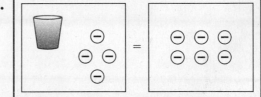

3.
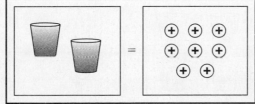

4.
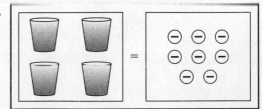

Draw an equation mat for each equation.

5. $3x = -9$

6. $x + (-1) = 7$

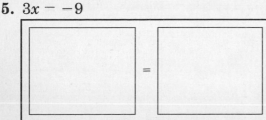

Modeling Mathematics

Solving One-Step Equations

Equation mats, cups, and counters can be used to model equations. The cups are used to represent an unknown number of positive or negative counters. Study the diagrams below.

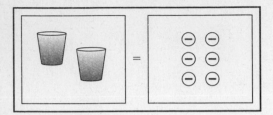   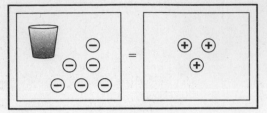

On the left side of the mat, the two cups represent two unknown values or $2x$. The right side of the mat has six negative counters representing -6. The equation represented on this mat is $2x = -6$.

On the left side of the mat, the cup represents an unknown value x and the six negative counters represent -6. Therefore, the left side of the mat represents $x + (-6)$. The three positive counters on the right side of the mat represent 3. The equation represented on this mat is $x + (-6) = 3$.

Write an equation for each equation mat.

1.
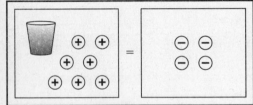

$$x + 7 = -4$$

2.
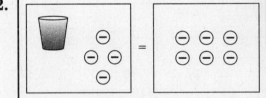

$$x + (-4) = -6$$

3.
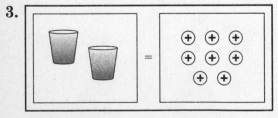

$$2x = 8$$

4.

$$4x = -8$$

Draw an equation mat for each equation.

5. $3x = -9$
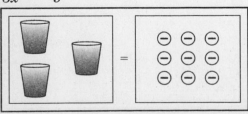

6. $x + (-1) = 7$
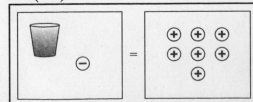

Algebra 1

Modeling Mathematics

Solving Multi-Step Equations

Some equations cannot be solved in one step. These types of equations can also be modeled on an equation mat. Study the equation below.

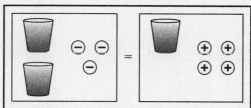

On the left side of the mat, the two cups represent two unknown values, or $2x$. The three negative counters represent -3. So, the left side of the mat represents $2x + (-3)$. On the right side of the mat, the cup represents an unknown value x, and the four positive counters represent 4. The equation represented on this mat is $2x + (-3) = x + 4$.

Write an equation for each equation mat.

1.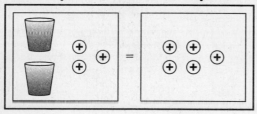

2.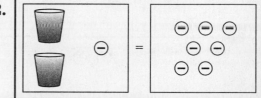

3.

4.

Draw an equation mat for each equation.

5. $3x + 2 = -4$

6. $3x + (-1) = 2x$

Algebra 1

Modeling Mathematics

Solving Multi-Step Equations

Some equations cannot be solved in one step. These types of equations can also be modeled on an equation mat. Study the equation below.

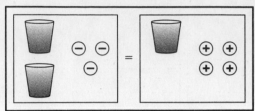

On the left side of the mat, the two cups represent two unknown values, or $2x$. The three negative counters represent -3. So, the left side of the mat represents $2x + (-3)$. On the right side of the mat, the cup represents an unknown value x, and the four positive counters represent 4. The equation represented on this mat is $2x + (-3) = x + 4$.

Write an equation for each equation mat.

1.
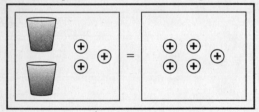

$$2x + 3 = 5$$

2.
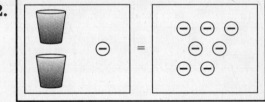

$$2x + (-1) = -7$$

3.

$$2x = x + (-5)$$

4.

$$2x + 2 = x + (-3)$$

Draw an equation mat for each equation.

5. $3x + 2 = -4$

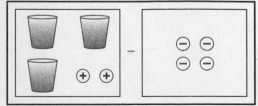

6. $3x + (-1) = 2x$

Modeling Mathematics

Ratios

Use the length of your head as one unit to measure the body parts listed in the first column. Record the relationship, or ratio, of each of the parts you measured to your head.

Length of your head: _____

Measurement	Length in Inches	Length in Heads	Ratio to Your Head
Total Height			
Waist to Hip			
Ankle to Bottom of Bare Heel			
Elbow to Wrist			
Shoulder to Tip of Finger			
Chin to Waist			
Knee to Ankle			
Underarm to Elbow			
Wrist to Tip of Finger			

Modeling Mathematics

Ratios

Use the length of your head as one unit to measure the body parts listed in the first column. Record the relationship, or ratio, of each of the parts you measured to your head.

Length of your head: _____

Measurement	Length in Inches	Length in Heads	Ratio to Your Head
Total Height			
Waist to Hip			
Ankle to Bottom of Bare Heel			
Elbow to Wrist			
Shoulder to Tip of Finger			
Chin to Waist			
Knee to Ankle			
Underarm to Elbow			
Wrist to Tip of Finger			

Modeling Mathematics

Slope

Use a geoboard to find the slope of each segment whose endpoints are at the coordinates given below. Draw a picture to show how you placed the three rubber bands on the geoboard to find the slope.

1. (1, 3) and (5, 4)

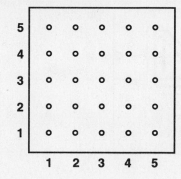

2. (2, 3) and (4, 5)

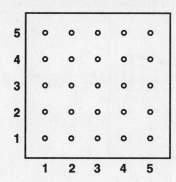

3. (2, 1) and (5, 5)

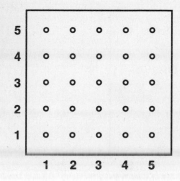

4. (2, 5) and (1, 2)

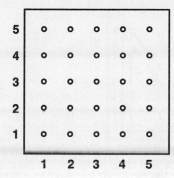

5. (4, 1) and (2, 2)

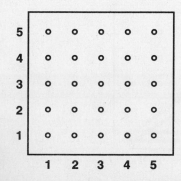

6. (2, 3) and (5, 1)

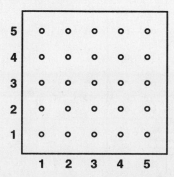

Modeling Mathematics

Slope

Use a geoboard to find the slope of each segment whose endpoints are at the coordinates given below. Draw a picture to show how you placed the three rubber bands on the geoboard to find the slope.

1. (1, 3) and (5, 4) $\dfrac{1}{4}$

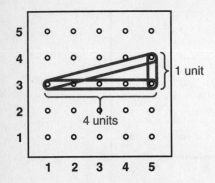

2. (2, 3) and (4, 5) $\dfrac{2}{2} = 1$

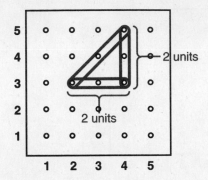

3. (2, 1) and (5, 5) $\dfrac{4}{3}$

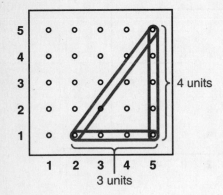

4. (2, 5) and (1, 2) $\dfrac{3}{1} = 3$

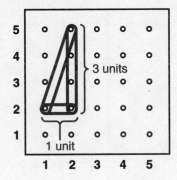

5. (4, 1) and (2, 2) $-\dfrac{1}{2}$

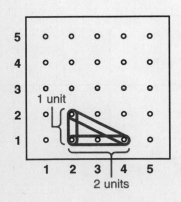

6. (2, 3) and (5, 1) $-\dfrac{2}{3}$

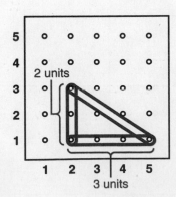

Modeling Mathematics

Solving Inequalities

Model the solution for each inequality. Draw a picture to show each step of your solution. Write the inequality that describes each step.

1. $3x > 9$

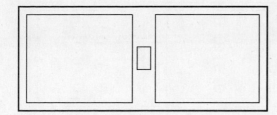

_____

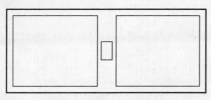

_____

2. $4x < -8$

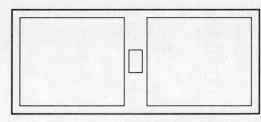

_____

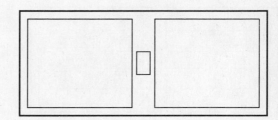

_____

3. $-4x < 4$

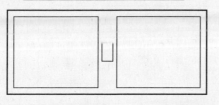

_____

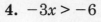

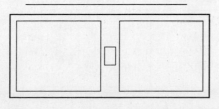

_____

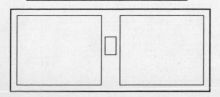

_____

4. $-3x > -6$

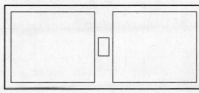

_____

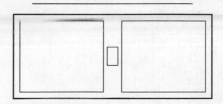

_____

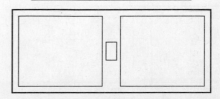

_____

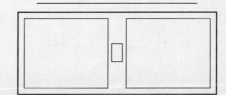

_____

Modeling Mathematics

Solving Inequalities

Model the solution for each inequality. Draw a picture to show each step of your solution. Write the inequality that describes each step.

1. $3x > 9$

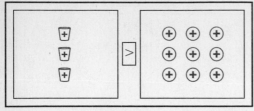

$$\underline{\hspace{2em} 3x > 9 \hspace{2em}}$$

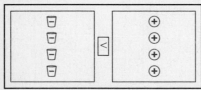

$$\underline{\hspace{2em} x > 3 \hspace{2em}}$$

2. $4x < -8$

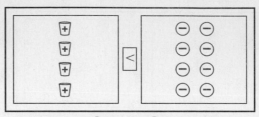

$$\underline{\hspace{2em} 4x < -8 \hspace{2em}}$$

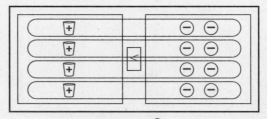

$$\underline{\hspace{2em} x < -2 \hspace{2em}}$$

3. $-4x < 4$

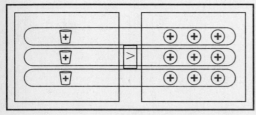

$$\underline{\hspace{2em} -4x < 4 \hspace{2em}}$$

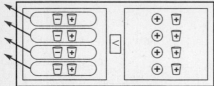

$$\underline{\hspace{2em} 0 < 4 + 4x \hspace{2em}}$$

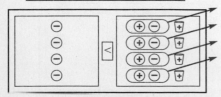

$$\underline{\hspace{2em} -4 < 4x \hspace{2em}}$$

$$\underline{\hspace{2em} -1 < x \hspace{2em}}$$

4. $-3x > -6$

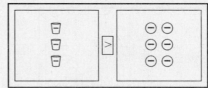

$$\underline{\hspace{2em} -3x > -6 \hspace{2em}}$$

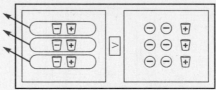

$$\underline{\hspace{2em} 0 > -6 + 3x \hspace{2em}}$$

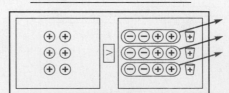

$$\underline{\hspace{2em} 6 > 3x \hspace{2em}}$$

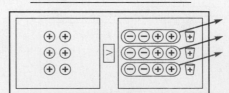

$$\underline{\hspace{2em} 2 > x \hspace{2em}}$$

Polynomials

Use algebra tiles to model each monomial or polynomial. Then draw a diagram of your model.

1. $-3x^2$

2. $2x^2 - 3x + 5$

3. $2x^2 - 7$

4. $6x - 4$

Write each model as an algebraic expression.

5.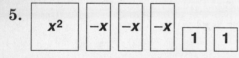

   _____

6.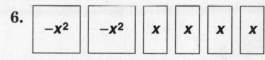

   _____

7.

| x^2 | x^2 | $-x$ | -1 | -1 | -1 | -1 | -1 |

   _____

8.

| $-x^2$ | x | x | x | -1 |

   _____

9. Write a few sentences giving reasons why algebra tiles are sometimes called *area tiles*.

   _____

   _____

   _____

Modeling Mathematics

Polynomials

Use algebra tiles to model each monomial or polynomial. Then draw a diagram of your model.

1. $-3x^2$

2. $2x^2 - 3x + 5$

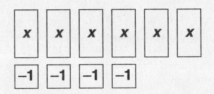

3. $2x^2 - 7$

4. $6x - 4$

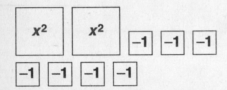

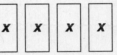

Write each model as an algebraic expression.

5.

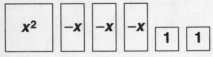

$\underline{x^2 - 3x + 2}$

6.

$\underline{-2x^2 + 4x}$

7.

$\underline{2x^2 - x - 5}$

8.

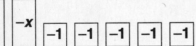

$\underline{-x^2 + 3x - 1}$

9. Write a few sentences giving reasons why algebra tiles are sometimes called *area tiles*.

$\underline{x^2,\ x,\ \text{and 1 represent the areas of the tiles.}}$

_____

_____

NAME_____ DATE _____

Student Edition
Pages 520–521

Modeling Mathematics

Adding and Subtracting Polynomials

Use algebra tiles to find each sum or difference.

1. $(2x^2 - 7x + 6) + (-3x^2 + 7x)$

_____

2. $(-2x^2 + 3x) + (-7x - 2)$

_____

3. $(x^2 - 4x) - (3x^2 + 2x)$

_____

4. $(3x^2 - 5x - 2) - (x^2 - x + 1)$

_____

Is each statement true or false? Justify your answer with a drawing.

5. $(3x^2 + 2x - 4) + (-x^2 + 2x - 3) = 2x^3 + 4x - 7$

_____

6. $(x^2 - 2x) - (-3x^2 + 4x - 3) = -2x^2 - 6x - 3$

_____

7. Find $(x^2 - 2x + 4) - (4x + 3)$ using each method from Activity 2 and Activity 4. Illustrate with drawings and explain in writing how zero-pairs are used in each case.

_____

_____

Modeling Mathematics

Adding and Subtracting Polynomials

Use algebra tiles to find each sum or difference.

1. $(2x^2 - 7x + 6) + (-3x^2 + 7x)$

   $-x^2 + 6$

2. $(-2x^2 + 3x) + (-7x - 2)$

   $-2x^2 - 4x - 2$

3. $(x^2 - 4x) - (3x^2 + 2x)$

   $-2x^2 - 6x$

4. $(3x^2 - 5x - 2) - (x^2 - x + 1)$

   $2x^2 - 4x - 3$

Is each statement true or false? Justify your answer with a drawing.

5. $(3x^2 + 2x - 4) + (-x^2 + 2x - 3) = 2x^2 + 4x - 7$

   true

6. $(x^2 - 2x) - (-3x^2 + 4x - 3) = -2x^2 - 6x - 3$

   false

7. Find $(x^2 - 2x + 4) - (4x + 3)$ using each method from Activity 2 and Activity 4. Illustrate with drawings and explain in writing how zero-pairs are used in each case.

   Method from Activity 2: You need to add zero-pairs so that you can remove 4 green *x*-tiles.

   Method from Activity 4: You remove all zero-pairs to find the difference in simplest form.

_____

_____

Multiplying a Polynomial by a Monomial

Use algebra tiles to find each product.

1. $x(x + 2)$

_____

2. $x(x - 3)$

_____

3. $2x(x + 1)$

_____

4. $2x(x - 3)$

_____

5. $x(2x + 1)$

_____

6. $3x(2x - 1)$

_____

Is each statement true or false? Justify your answer with a drawing.

7. $x(2x + 4) = 2x^2 + 4x$

_____

8. $2x(3x - 4) = 6x^2 - 8$

_____

9. Suppose you have a square storage building that measures x feet on a side. You triple the length of the building and increase the width by 15 feet.

   a. What will be the dimensions of the new building?

   _____

   b. What is the area of the new building? Write your solution in paragraph form, complete with drawings.

   _____

   _____

   _____

Modeling Mathematics

Multiplying a Polynomial by a Monomial

Use algebra tiles to find each product.

1. $x(x + 2)$

$$x^2 + 2x$$

2. $x(x - 3)$

$$x^2 - 3x$$

3. $2x(x + 1)$

$$2x^2 + 2x$$

4. $2x(x - 3)$

$$2x^2 - 6x$$

5. $x(2x + 1)$

$$2x^2 + x$$

6. $3x(2x - 1)$

$$6x^2 - 3x$$

Is each statement true or false? Justify your answer with a drawing.

7. $x(2x + 4) = 2x^2 + 4x$

true

8. $2x(3x - 4) = 6x^2 - 8$

false

9. Suppose you have a square storage building that measures x feet on a side. You triple the length of the building and increase the width by 15 feet.

a. What will be the dimensions of the new building?

$3x$ and $x + 15$

b. What is the area of the new building? Write your solution in paragraph form, complete with drawings.

$3x^2 + 45x$ square feet

Modeling Mathematics

Multiplying Polynomials

Use algebra tiles to find each product.

1. $(x + 1)(x + 2)$

   _____

2. $(x + 1)(x - 3)$

   _____

3. $(x - 2)(x - 4)$

   _____

4. $(x + 1)(2x + 2)$

   _____

5. $(x - 1)(2x + 2)$

   _____

6. $(x - 3)(2x - 1)$

   _____

Is each statement true or false? Justify your answer with a drawing.

7. $(x + 4)(x + 6) = x^2 + 24$

   _____

8. $(x + 3)(x - 2) = x^2 + x - 6$

   _____

9. $(x - 1)(x + 5) = x^2 - 4x - 5$

   _____

10. $(x - 2)(x - 3) = x^2 - 5x + 6$

    _____

11. You can also use the distributive property to find the product of two binomials. The figure at the right shows the model for $(x + 3)(x + 2)$ separated into four parts. Write a paragraph explaining how this model shows the use of the distributive property.

_____

_____

_____

_____

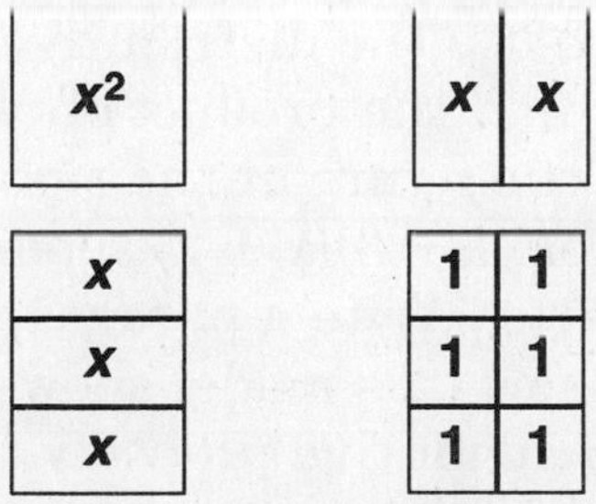

NAME_____ DATE _____

Modeling Mathematics

Multiplying Polynomials

Use algebra tiles to find each product.

1. $(x + 1)(x + 2)$

_____$x^2 + 3x + 2$_____

2. $(x + 1)(x - 3)$

_____$x^2 - 2x - 3$_____

3. $(x - 2)(x - 4)$

_____$x^2 - 6x + 8$_____

4. $(x + 1)(2x + 2)$

_____$2x^2 + 4x + 2$_____

5. $(x - 1)(2x + 2)$

_____$2x^2 - 2$_____

6. $(x - 3)(2x - 1)$

_____$2x^2 - 7x + 3$_____

Is each statement true or false? Justify your answer with a drawing.

7. $(x + 4)(x + 6) = x^2 + 24$

_____**false**_____

8. $(x + 3)(x - 2) = x^2 + x - 6$

_____**true**_____

9. $(x - 1)(x + 5) = x^2 - 4x - 5$

_____**false**_____

10. $(x - 2)(x - 3) = x^2 - 5x + 6$

_____**true**_____

11. You can also use the distributive property to find the product of two binomials. The figure at the right shows the model for $(x + 3)(x + 2)$ separated into four parts. Write a paragraph explaining how this model shows the use of the distributive property.

By the distributive property,
_____

$(x + 3)(x + 2) = x(x + 2) + 3(x + 2)$.
_____

The top row represents $x(x + 2)$ or $x^2 + 2x$. The
_____

bottom row represents $3(x + 2)$ or $3x + 6$.
_____

Modeling Mathematics

Factoring Using the Distributive Property

Use algebra tiles to factor each binomial.

1. $2x + 4$

2. $4x + 6$

3. $3x - 9$

4. $4x - 10$

5. $x^2 + 2x$

6. $2x^2 + x$

7. $3x^2 + 6x$

8. $2x^2 + 4x$

9. $x^2 - x$

Tell whether each binomial can be factored. Justify your answer with a drawing.

10. $4x + 5$

11. $8 - 12x$

12. $4x^2 + 3$

13. $x^2 - 6x$

Modeling Mathematics

Factoring Using the Distributive Property

Use algebra tiles to factor each binomial.

1. $2x + 4$
   2(x + 2)

2. $4x + 6$
   2(2x + 3)

3. $3x - 9$
   3(x - 3)

4. $4x - 10$
   2(2x - 5)

5. $x^2 + 2x$
   x(x + 2)

6. $2x^2 + x$
   x(2x + 1)

7. $3x^2 + 6x$
   3x(x + 2)

8. $2x^2 + 4x$
   2x(x + 2)

9. $x^2 - x$
   x(x - 1)

Tell whether each binomial can be factored. Justify your answer with a drawing.

10. $4x + 5$ **no**

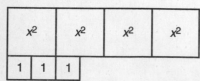

x	x	x	x

1	1	1	1	1

11. $8 - 12x$ **yes; 4(2 − 3x)**

1	1	−x	−x	−x
1	1	−x	−x	−x
1	1	−x	−x	−x
1	1	−x	−x	−x

12. $4x^2 + 3$ **no**

x^2	x^2	x^2	x^2

1	1	1

13. $x^2 - 6x$ **yes; x(x − 6)**

x^2	−x	−x	−x	−x	−x	−x

10-3A

Modeling Mathematics

Factoring Trinomials

Use algebra tiles to factor each trinomial.

1. $x^2 + 3x + 2$

2. $x^2 + 6x + 9$

3. $x^2 + 5x + 4$

4. $x^2 - 4x + 3$

5. $x^2 - 7x + 12$

6. $x^2 - 4x + 4$

7. $x^2 + x - 6$

8. $x^2 + 3x - 4$

9. $x^2 - 3x - 10$

Tell whether each trinomial can be factored. Justify your answer with a drawing.

10. $x^2 + x + 3$

11. $x^2 + 5x + 6$

12. $x^2 - 6x + 5$

13. $x^2 - 2x - 4$

Modeling Mathematics

Factoring Trinomials

Use algebra tiles to factor each trinomial.

1. $x^2 + 3x + 2$
(x + 2)(x + 1)

2. $x^2 + 6x + 9$
(x + 3)(x + 3)

3. $x^2 + 5x + 4$
(x + 4)(x + 1)

4. $x^2 - 4x + 3$
(x − 3)(x − 1)

5. $x^2 - 7x + 12$
(x − 4)(x − 3)

6. $x^2 - 4x + 4$
(x − 2)(x − 2)

7. $x^2 + x - 6$
(x + 3)(x − 2)

8. $x^2 + 3x - 4$
(x + 4)(x − 1)

9. $x^2 - 3x - 10$
(x − 5)(x + 2)

Tell whether each trinomial can be factored. Justify your answer with a drawing.

10. $x^2 + x + 3$ **no**

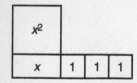

11. $x^2 + 5x + 6$ **yes; (x + 3)(x + 2)**

x^2	x	x
x	1	1
x	1	1
x	1	1

12. $x^2 - 6x + 5$ **yes; (x − 5)(x − 1)**

x^2	−x	−x	−x	−x	−x
−x	1	1	1	1	1

13. $x^2 - 2x - 4$ **no**

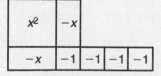

13-1A

Modeling Mathematics

The Pythagorean Theorem

Build squares on each side of the triangles shown below using a geoboard or dot paper. Record the areas of the squares.

1. _____

2. _____

3. _____

Draw a square on dot paper having each area.

4. 4 square units

5. 9 square units

6. 8 square units

7. 13 square units

8. 17 square units

9. 32 square units

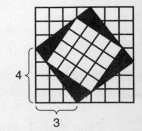

10. Write a paragraph explaining how to find the total area of the shaded triangles in the drawing at the right.

_____

_____

Modeling Mathematics

The Pythagorean Theorem

Build squares on each side of the triangles shown below. Record the areas of the squares.

1. **4 + 4 = 8**

2. **9 + 1 = 10**

3. **16 + 9 = 25**

Draw a square on dot paper having each area. **See students' drawings.**

4. 4 square units

5. 9 square units

6. 8 square units

7. 13 square units

8. 17 square units

9. 32 square units

10. Write a paragraph explaining how to find the total area of the shaded triangles in the drawing at the right.

The total area of the 4 triangles equals the area of the large square minus the area of the triangle in each corner minus the area of the small square; 49 − 4(6) − 16, or 9, square units.

NAME ______________________ DATE ____________

Modeling Mathematics

Student Edition
Page 742

Completing the Square

Use algebra tiles to complete the square for each equation.

1. $x^2 + 4x + 3 = 0$

2. $x^2 - 6x + 5 = 0$

3. $x^2 + 4x - 1 = 0$

4. $x^2 - 2x + 5 = 3$

5. $x^2 - 4x + 7 = 8$

6. $0 = x^2 + 8x - 3$

7. In the equations shown above, the coefficient of x was always an even number. Sometimes you have an equation like $x^2 + 3x - 1 = 0$ in which the coefficient of x is an odd number. Complete the square by making a drawing.

8. Write a paragraph explaining how you could complete the square with models without first rewriting the equation. Include a drawing.

____

____

____

____

Modeling Mathematics

Completing the Square

Use algebra tiles to complete the square for each equation.

1. $x^2 + 4x + 3 = 0$
$(x + 2)^2 = 1$

2. $x^2 - 6x + 5 = 0$
$(x - 3)^2 = 4$

3. $x^2 + 4x - 1 = 0$
$(x + 2)^2 = 5$

4. $x^2 - 2x + 5 = 3$
$(x - 1)^2 = -1$

5. $x^2 - 4x + 7 = 8$
$(x - 2)^2 = 5$

6. $0 = x^2 + 8x - 3$
$(x + 4)^2 = 19$

7. In the equations shown above, the coefficient of x was always an even number. Sometimes you have an equation like $x^2 + 3x - 1 = 0$ in which the coefficient of x is an odd number. Complete the square by making a drawing.
$(x + 1.5)^2 = 3.25$

8. Write a paragraph explaining how you could complete the square with models without first rewriting the equation. Include a drawing.

Sample answer: You could model the expression

on one side of the mat. Then add the appropriate

1-tiles needed to complete the square to each

side of the mat.

Modeling Mathematics Activity
Teaching Suggestions

Multiplying and Dividing Rational Numbers

Objective

Examine the rules for multiplying and dividing rational numbers.

Materials Needed

- Classroom set of 2-7 Modeling Mathematics Activity
  (p. 38 in this booklet)
- Transparency from 2-7 Modeling Mathematics Activity
  (p. 37 in this booklet)
- Video Camera
- VCR
- TV

Implementation

1. Videotape students moving forward and backward for several minutes each way. (You may choose to do this before class.)

2. Display the transparency on the overhead projector revealing one rule at a time.

3. Play the videotape corresponding to the rule displayed and discuss rational number products and quotients.

4. Students should notice that since the length of the tape playing forward or backward had no effect on the resultant motion, neither will the magnitude of the numbers affect the sign of the products.

5. Ask students for a general rule for multiplying and dividing rational numbers. (That is, same signs = positive, different signs = negative.)

6. Assign the worksheet as a group or individual activity.

Modeling Mathematics Activity

Multiplying and Dividing Rational Numbers

Move forward (+)	Play tape forward (+)	= Forward motion (+)

Move forward (+)	Play tape backward (−)	= Backward motion (−)
	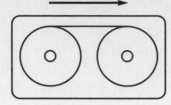	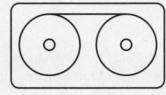

Move backward (−)	Play tape forward (+)	= Backward motion (−)
	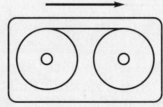	

Move backward (−)	Play tape backward (−)	= Forward motion (+)
	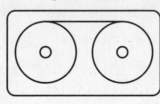	

Multiply.

$(+14)(+20) = $ _____ $(+8)(-12) = $ _____

$(-25)(+6) = $ _____ $(-9)(-40) = $ _____

$\left(-\dfrac{1}{2}\right)(+62) = $ _____ $(+2.4)(-0.5) = $ _____

37   *Algebra 1*

2-7

Modeling Mathematics Activity

Multiplying and Dividing Rational Numbers

In groups, act out, videotape, and play back each product.

1. $4(-1)$ **2.** $5(-2)$ **3.** $(-3)(+4)$

4. What is the sign of the answer for each problem? _____

5. State the rules for multiplying rational numbers. _____

_____

Multiply or divide.

6. $(+25)(+12) =$ _____   **7.** $(-3.2)(+1.5) =$ _____

8. $(-25)(0.5) =$ _____   **9.** $(+7)(+49) =$ _____

10. $\left(-\dfrac{1}{4}\right)(+64) =$ _____   **11.** $\left(-\dfrac{3}{8}\right)\left(-\dfrac{24}{9}\right) =$ _____

12. $(10)(-40) =$ _____   **13.** $(44)(11) =$ _____

14. $(90)\left(\dfrac{1}{4}\right) =$ _____   **15.** $(-3)(-6)(-1) =$ _____

16. $(-25) \div (5) =$ _____   **17.** $(4.5) \div (0.9) =$ _____

18. $(+6) \div (-3) =$ _____   **19.** $\left(-\dfrac{1}{2}\right) \div \left(-\dfrac{3}{8}\right) =$ _____

20. Suppose you wrote 4 checks for $5.00. How much money did _____
you spend?

     Is your answer a positive or negative number?   _____

21. Taylor High School's defensive lineman sacked North High   _____
School's quarterback in 3 consecutive plays for lost yardage of
8 yards each play. How far behind the line of scrimmage is
North High School?

     Is the lost yardage a positive or negative number?   _____

22. During the 4 day U.S. Open Golf Tournament, Jack   _____
Nicklaus finished 2 under par each day. What number
represented Jack's score at the end of the tournament?

23. Mr. Muscle lost $8540 gambling in Las Vegas. He won back   _____
one-half of his losses the following day. What were Mr. Muscle's
net winnings or losses? (Represent your answer with a positive
or negative number.)

Modeling Mathematics Activity

Multiplying and Dividing Rational Numbers

In groups, act out, videotape, and play back each product.

1. $4(-1)$ **−4**
2. $5(-2)$ **−10**
3. $(-3)(+4)$ **−12**

4. What is the sign of the answer for each problem? **negative**

5. State the rules for multiplying rational numbers. _____
   $(+)(+) = (+), (+)(-) = (-), (-)(-) = (+)$

Multiply or divide.

6. $(+25)(+12) =$ **300**

7. $(-3.2)(+1.5) =$ **−4.80**

8. $(-25)(0.5) =$ **−12.5**

9. $(+7)(+49) =$ **343**

10. $\left(-\frac{1}{4}\right)(+64) =$ **−16**

11. $\left(-\frac{3}{8}\right)\left(-\frac{24}{9}\right) =$ **1**

12. $(10)(-40) =$ **−400**

13. $(44)(11) =$ **484**

14. $(90)\left(\frac{1}{4}\right) =$ **22.5**

15. $(-3)(-6)(-1) =$ **−18**

16. $(-25) \div (5) =$ **−5**

17. $(4.5) \div (0.9) =$ **5**

18. $(+6) \div (-3) =$ **−2**

19. $\left(-\frac{1}{2}\right) \div \left(-\frac{3}{8}\right) =$ **$\frac{4}{3}$**

20. Suppose you wrote 4 checks for $5.00. How much money did you spend? **$20**

    Is your answer a positive or negative number? **neg.**

21. Taylor High School's defensive lineman sacked North High School's quarterback in 3 consecutive plays for lost yardage of 8 yards each play. How far behind the line of scrimmage is North High School? **24 yd**

    Is the lost yardage a positive or negative number? **neg.**

22. During the 4 day U.S. Open Golf Tournament, Jack Nicklaus finished 2 under par each day. What number represented Jack's score at the end of the tournament? **−8**

23. Mr. Muscle lost $8540 gambling in Las Vegas. He won back one-half of his losses the following day. What were Mr. Muscle's net winnings or losses? (Represent your answer with a positive or negative number.) **−$4270**

Modeling Mathematics Activity
Teaching Suggestions

Formulas

Objectives

Develop, understand, and use formulas.

Improve spatial visualization skills.

Materials Needed

- Classroom set of 2-9 Modeling Mathematics Activity (p. 41 in this booklet)

- Transparency from 2-9 Modeling Mathematics Activity (p. 40 in this booklet)

Preparation

Cut the transparency on the dashed lines and color triangles A, B, and C if you wish.

Implementation

1. In groups, have students complete questions 1 and 2 on the worksheet.

2. Display the grid and figures 1–12 on the overhead projector. Discuss student strategies for finding areas.

3. Place triangle A over figure 1 and triangle B over figure 2. Have students compare their areas.

4. Put figures 1–12 over the grid. Ask students to find the altitude of each triangle. Ask students how to find the altitude of an obtuse triangle.

5. Now remove figures 1–12 and put triangles A, B, and C on the grid. Draw conclusions and write formulas for the area of a rectangle, a parallelogram, and a triangle.

6. In groups, have students complete questions 3 and 4. Groups can trade question 4 with other groups to compare answers.

Modeling Mathematics Activity

Formulas

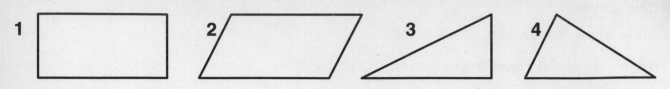

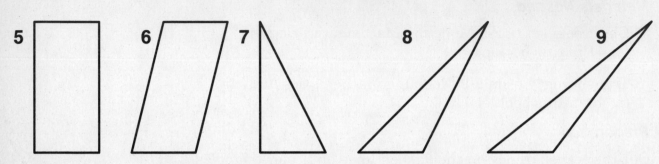

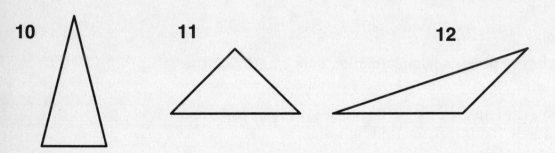

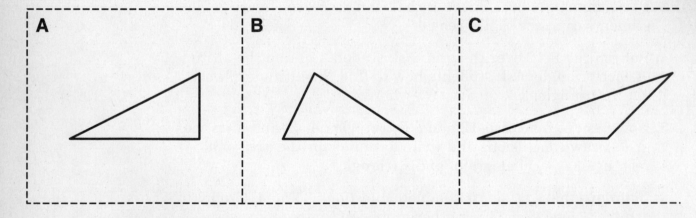

Modeling Mathematics Activity

Formulas

1. Estimate the area of each figure below. Write your estimate inside the figure.

2. How do the areas of the triangles compare with the areas of the parallelograms? How do the base and height of each triangle compare with the base and height of each parallelogram? What conclusions can you make?

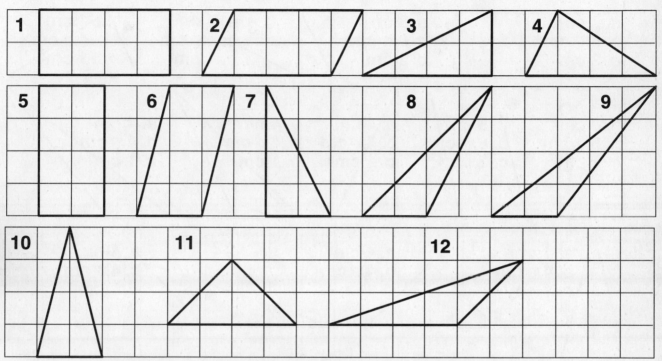

3. Using the formulas you developed for the area of a parallelogram and a triangle, find the area of each figure above when the scale of the grid is **a.** 1 unit = 1 cm; **b.** 1 unit = x cm; and **c.** 1 unit = 0.5 cm.

4. On the grid below, draw a rectangle, parallelogram, acute triangle, right triangle, and obtuse triangle with different measures for their bases and heights. Find the area of each figure.

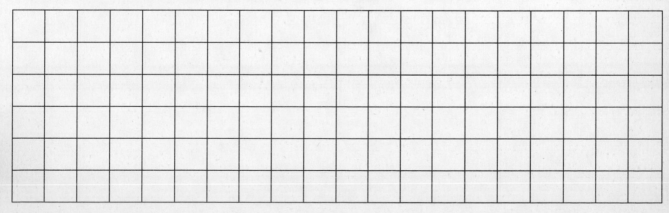

Formulas

1. Estimate the area of each figure below. Write your estimate inside the figure. **Estimates may vary.**

2. How do the areas of the triangles compare with the areas of the parallelograms? How do the base and height of each triangle compare with the base and height of each parallelogram? What conclusions can you make? **For base *b* and height *h*, area of parallelogram = *bh*, area of a triangle = $\frac{1}{2}bh$.**

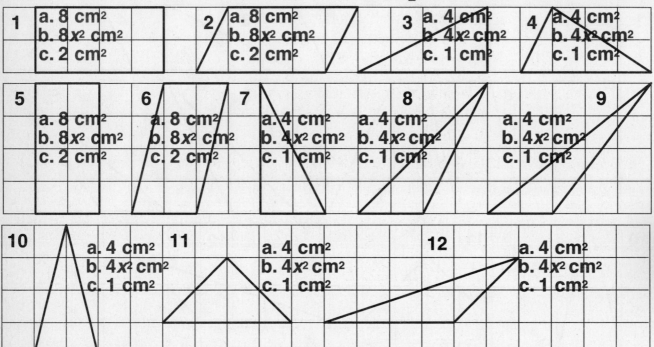

1	a. 8 cm²	2	a. 8 cm²	3	a. 4 cm²	4	a. 4 cm²
	b. 8x^2 cm²		b. 8x^2 cm²		b. 4x^2 cm²		b. 4x^2 cm²
	c. 2 cm²		c. 2 cm²		c. 1 cm²		c. 1 cm²

5	6	7	8	9
a. 8 cm²	a. 8 cm²	a. 4 cm²	a. 4 cm²	a. 4 cm²
b. 8x^2 cm²	b. 8x^2 cm²	b. 4x^2 cm²	b. 4x^2 cm²	b. 4x^2 cm²
c. 2 cm²	c. 2 cm²	c. 1 cm²	c. 1 cm²	c. 1 cm²

10	a. 4 cm²	11	a. 4 cm²	12	a. 4 cm²
	b. 4x^2 cm²		b. 4x^2 cm²		b. 4x^2 cm²
	c. 1 cm²		c. 1 cm²		c. 1 cm²

3. Using the formulas you developed for the area of a parallelogram and a triangle, find the area of each figure above when the scale of the grid is **a.** 1 unit = 1 cm; **b.** 1 unit = *x* cm; and **c.** 1 unit = 0.5 cm. **Answers provided within or near each figure.**

4. On the grid below, draw a rectangle, parallelogram, acute triangle, right triangle, and obtuse triangle with different measures for their bases and heights. Find the area of each figure. **Answers may vary.**

Modeling Mathematics Activity
Teaching Suggestions

Solving Equations

Objectives

Determine order of operations of an algebraic sentence.
Solve equations using inverse operations.
Solve equations with more than one operation.

Materials Needed

- Classroom set of 3-3 Modeling Mathematics Activity
  (p. 44 in this booklet)
- Transparency from 3-3 Modeling Mathematics Activity
  (p. 43 in this booklet)
- Small object
- Box for object
- Wrapping paper
- Ribbon

Preparation

Prepare an object, box, wrapping paper, and ribbon for each group
of students. Cut the transparency on the dashed lines.

Implementation

1. Have groups of students wrap the object while one member of
   each group records the steps of the process.

2. Have the recorder read the steps backwards or in *inverse* order
   while the other students unwrap the package.

3. Discuss how the forward and reverse process applies to solving
   algebraic equations, making sure to identify order of operations
   as a requirement for wrapping the x. Have students complete
   exercises 1–3. Ask students: What was done to x? What was
   done to undo x?

4. Use the transparency models to demonstrate solving simple
   equations using a "wrap and unwrap x" strategy. Stress inverse
   operations to unwrap x from the equation.

5. Show algebraic solutions to equations without using models.

6. In groups, have students complete the worksheet.

Modeling Mathematics Activity

Solving Equations

  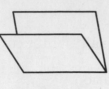  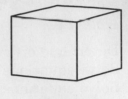

TOY   BOX   WRAPPING PAPER   RIBBON   PRESENT

Wrap a gift

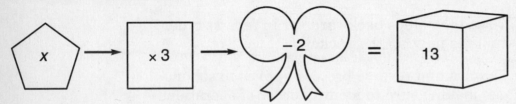

Unwrap a gift

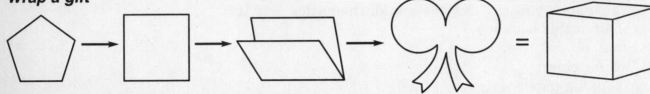

Wrap an x algebraically

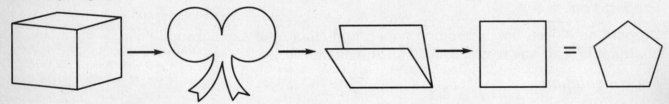

Unwrap x using inverse operations

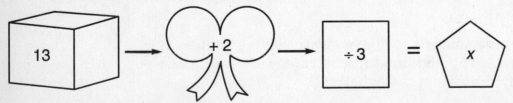

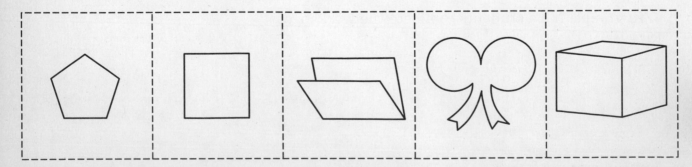

Algebra 1

Solving Equations

Example:

x → $\times 2$ = 8 What must be done to unwrap x? __**Divide by 2.**__

8 → $\div 2$ = x What is x? __**4**__

1. x → -6 = 4

What must be done to unwrap x? _____   What is x? _____

2. x → $\times 4$ → -1 = 23

What must be done to unwrap x? _____   What is x? _____

3. x → -3 , $\div 2$ → $+5$ = 9

What must be done to unwrap x? _____   What is x? _____

Write a wrapping process for each equation.

Example $x + 4 = 0$

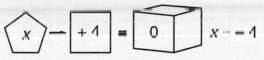
x → $+4$ = 0 $x = -4$

Example $3x - 4 = 8$

x , $\times 3$ → -4 = 8 $x = 4$

4. $x - 7 = 8$ _____ $x =$ _____

5. $x + 10 = -2$ _____ $x =$ _____

6. $x + 6 = 6$ _____ $x =$ _____

7. $2x = 20$ _____ $x =$ _____

8. $\frac{1}{3}x = 1$ _____ $x =$ _____

9. $2x - 1 = 5$ _____ $x =$ _____

10. $4x + 8 = 32$ _____ $x =$ _____

NAME_____ DATE _____

Modeling Mathematics Activity

Solving Equations

Example:

What must be done to unwrap x? **Divide by 2.**   What is x? **4**

1.

What must be done to unwrap x? **Add 6.**   What is x? **10**

2.

What must be done to unwrap x? **Add 1 and divide by 4.**   What is x? **6**

3.

What must be done to unwrap x? **Subtract 5, multiply by 2, and add 3.**   What is x? **11**

Write a wrapping process for each equation.

Example $x + 4 = 0$

$x = -4$

Example $3x - 4 = 8$

$x = 4$

4. $x - 7 = 8$ $x =$ **15**

5. $x + 10 = -2$ $x =$ **−12**

6. $x + 6 = 6$ $x =$ **0**

7. $2x = 20$ $x =$ **10**

8. $\frac{1}{3}x = 1$ $x =$ **3**

9. $2x - 1 = 5$ $x =$ **3**

10. $4x + 8 = 32$ $x =$ **6**

     Algebra 1

Modeling Mathematics Activity
Teaching Suggestions

Mixture Problems

Objective

Solve mixture problems using diagrams and charts to organize information.

Materials Needed

- Classroom set of 4-7 Modeling Mathematics Activity (p. 47 in this booklet)
- Transparency from 4-7 Modeling Mathematics Activity (p. 46 in this booklet)

Preparation

Cut the transparency on the dashed lines and color Figures 1, 2, and 3 if you wish.

Implementation

1. Display the transparency on the overhead projector and examine the mixture problem.

2. Let Figure 1 represent 9 pounds of $6.40/lb coffee and Figure 2 represent n pounds of $7.28/lb coffee. Place Figures 1 and 2 on the diagram as shown in the chart below.

3. Then place Figure 3 on the diagram to show that the mixture contains $(9 + n)$ pounds of coffee selling for $6.95 per pound.

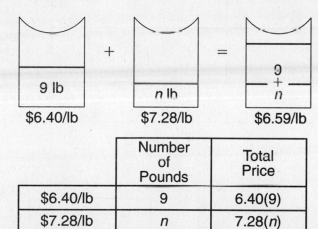

	Number of Pounds	Total Price
$6.40/lb	9	6.40(9)
$7.28/lb	n	7.28(n)
$6.59/lb	$9 + n$	6.59($9 + n$)

$$6.40(9) + 7.28n = 6.96(9 + n)$$
$$n = 15$$

4. Complete the chart. Discuss how to select necessary information and set up a mixture problem.

5. Practice some problems from Lesson 4-7 using the transparency.

6. In groups, have students complete the worksheet.

Modeling Mathematics Activity

Transparency Master

Mixture Problems

Cathy's Coffee Cafe sells gourmet coffee mixes by the pound. How many pounds of $7.28/lb coffee must Cathy mix with 9 pounds of $6.40/lb coffee to create a mixture worth $6.95 per pound?

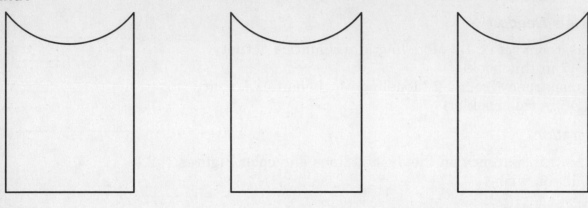

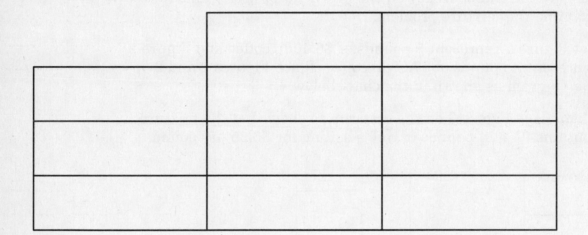

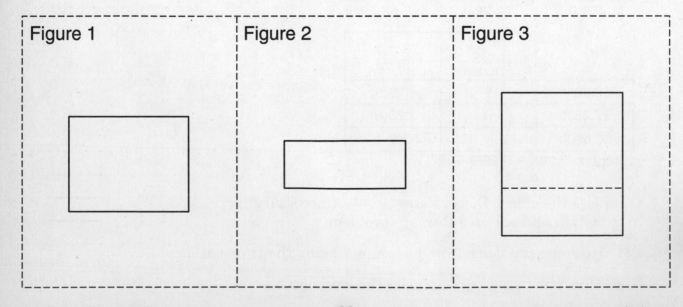

Figure 1

Figure 2

Figure 3

NAME_____ DATE _____

Modeling Mathematics Activity

Mixture Problems

Illustrate each problem using the diagrams below. Then complete the chart, write an equation, and solve each problem.

1. Nancy's Nut Shop sells cashews for $3.10 per pound and peanuts for $1.95 per pound. How many pounds of peanuts must be added to 15 pounds of cashews to make a mix that sells for $2.70 per pound?

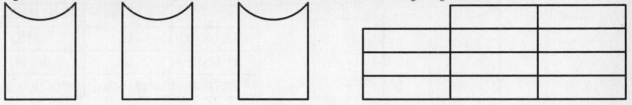

2. Anna has 4 times as many nickels as dimes in her bank. Her bank contains $7.20. How many nickels and dimes are in Anna's bank?

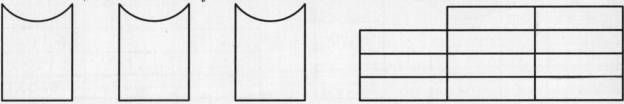

3. Carmen sold play tickets. Each adult ticket cost $4.00 and each student ticket cost $2.00. The total number of tickets sold was 260, and the total income was $700.00. How many of each kind of ticket were sold?

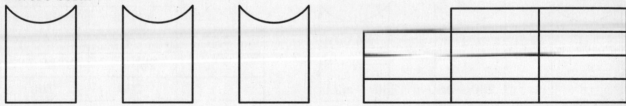

4. David sold carnival tickets for his school fund raiser. Adult tickets cost $2.50 and student tickets cost $1.50. If David collected $396.00 selling twice as many student tickets as adult tickets, how many of each kind of ticket did he sell?

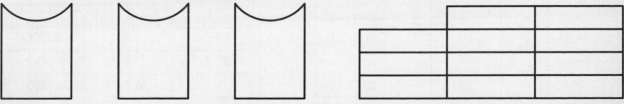

Mixture Problems

Illustrate each problem using the diagrams below. Then complete the chart, write an equation, and solve each problem.

1. Nancy's Nut Shop sells cashews for $3.10 per pound and peanuts for $1.95 per pound. How many pounds of peanuts must be added to 15 pounds of cashews to make a mix that sells for $2.70 per pound?

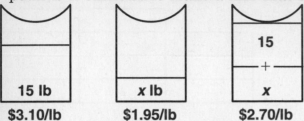

	# of lbs.	Total Price
$3.10/lb	15	3.10(15)
$1.95/lb	x	1.95(x)
$2.70/lb	15 + x	2.70(15 + x)

15 lb x lb x
$3.10/lb $1.95/lb $2.70/lb

$(3.10)(15) + (1.95)x = (2.70)(15 + x)$, **8 pounds of peanuts**

2. Anna has 4 times as many nickels as dimes in her bank. Her bank contains $7.20. How many nickels and dimes are in Anna's bank?

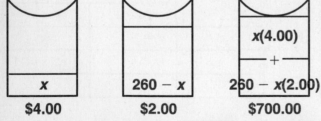

	# of coins	Total Amount
0.10	x	(0.10)(x)
0.05	4x	(0.05)(4x)
	x + 4x	$7.20

x 4x 4x(0.05)
0.10¢   0.05¢ $7.20

$(0.10)x + (0.05)(4x) = 7.20$, **96 nickels and 54 dimes**

3. Carmen sold play tickets. Each adult ticket cost $4.00 and each student ticket cost $2.00. The total number of tickets sold was 260, and the total income was $700.00. How many of each kind of ticket were sold?

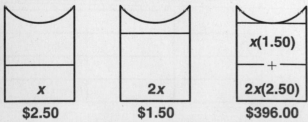

	# of Tix.	Total Amount
4.00	x	4x
2.00	260 − x	2(260 − x)
	260	700

x 260 − x 260 − x(2.00)
$4.00 $2.00 $700.00

$4x + (2)(260 − x) = 700$, **90 @ $4 and 170 @ $2**

4. David sold carnival tickets for his school fund raiser. Adult tickets cost $2.50 and student tickets cost $1.50. If David collected $396.00 selling twice as many student tickets as adult tickets, how many of each kind of ticket did he sell?

	# of Tix.	Total Amount
$2.50	x	2.50(x)
$1.50	2x	1.50(2x)
	x + 2x	396

x 2x 2x(2.50)
$2.50 $1.50 $396.00

$(2.50)x + (1.50)2x = 396$, **72 adult tickets and 144 student tickets**

Modeling Mathematics Activity
Teaching Suggestions

Functions

Objectives

Find functional values for a given function.
Write a linear equation given values for x and y.

Materials Needed

- Classroom set of 5-5 Modeling Mathematics Activity
  (p. 50 in this booklet)
- Transparency from 5-5 Modeling Mathematics Activity
  (p. 49 in this booklet)

Implementation

1. Display the transparency on the overhead projector.

2. Discuss the diagram of a function machine. The function rule is computed for each "x" input that yields "y" as its output.

3. Next, show the first line of examples where $f(x) = x + 2$.

4. Uncover the second line of function machines where $f(x) = 3x - 2$ and ask students for the values of y (the output).

5. Using the third line of function machines, assist students to develop the function rule $f(x) = 2x$ given the values in the table.

6. Play the *Function Machine Game* as follows. Player A thinks of a rule and acts as a function machine to compute a new number y from any x given to him or her. (Record x and y on a chart for each computation.) When a student wishes to guess the rule, she must first give an example for x and y. If correct, she may give the rule and write the equation. The winner of each round becomes player A and the game continues.

7. Use the worksheet for group or individual instruction.

Modeling Mathematics Activity

Functions

x	y

Function Machine

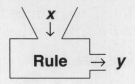

x	y
5	7
1	3
10	12

$f(x) = x + 2$

5 ↓
$x + 2$ → 7

1 ↓
$x + 2$ → 3

10 ↓
$x + 2$ → 12

x	y
1	
0	
3	

$f(x) = 3x - 2$

1 ↓
$3x - 2$ → y

0 ↓
$3x - 2$ → y

3 ↓
$3x - 2$ → y

x	y
4	8
−1	−2
3	6

$f(x) = ?$

4 ↓
→ 8

−1 ↓
→ −2

3 ↓
→ 6

NAME_____ DATE _____

Modeling Mathematics Activity

Functions

Find the rule for each function machine.

Example:

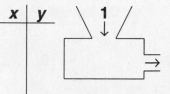

x	y
4	3
7	6
0	−1
−2	−3

$$y = x - 1$$

1.

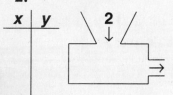

x	y

2.

x	y

3.

x	y

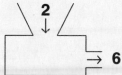

4.

x	y

5.

x	y

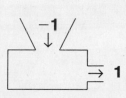 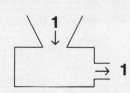 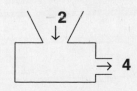 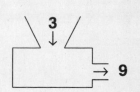

Algebra 1

Modeling Mathematics Activity

Functions

Find the rule for each function machine.

Example:

x	y
4	3
7	6
0	-1
-2	-3

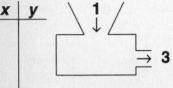

| 4 → 3 | 7 → 6 | 0 → -1 | -2 → -3 |

$$y = x - 1$$

1.

x	y

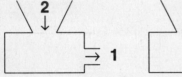

| 1 → 3 | -1 → -3 | 4 → 12 | 0 → 0 |

$$y = 3x$$

2.

x	y

| 2 → 1 | 6 → 3 | -4 → -2 | 1 → 0.5 |

$$y = 0.5x$$

3.

x	y

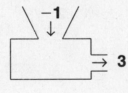

| 1 → 5 | -1 → 3 | 2 → 6 | -2 → 2 |

$$y = x + 4$$

4.

x	y

| 4 → 4 | -3 → 3 | 1 → -1 | -2 → 2 |

$$y = -x$$

5.

x	y

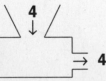
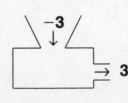
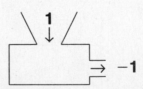

| -1 → 1 | 1 → 1 | -2 → 4 | 3 → 9 |

$$y = x^2$$

Modeling Mathematics Activity
Teaching Suggestions

Slopes of Parallel and Perpendicular Lines

Objectives

Discover the relationship between the slopes of parallel lines.
Discover the relationship between the slopes of perpendicular lines.

Materials Needed

- Classroom set of 6-6 Modeling Mathematics Activity
  (p. 53 in this booklet)
- Transparency from 6-6 Modeling Mathematics Activity
  (p. 52 in this booklet)
- Tracing paper
- Graph paper

Preparation

Cut the transparency on the dashed lines.

Implementation

1. Place lines a and b over the coordinate plane. Have students
   find their slopes and y-intercepts. Then, in groups, have
   students complete exercises 1 and 2 on the worksheet.

2. Discuss the relationship of the slopes of parallel lines.

3. Identify the slope-intercept form of a linear equation. Have
   students complete exercise 3.

4. In a similar manner, have students complete exercises 4–6.
   Discuss slopes of perpendicular lines and their equations using
   the exercises as a guide.

Extension

Construct parallelograms and write equations for the sides, using
parallel and/or perpendicular line models.

Modeling Mathematics Activity

Slopes of Parallel and Perpendicular Lines

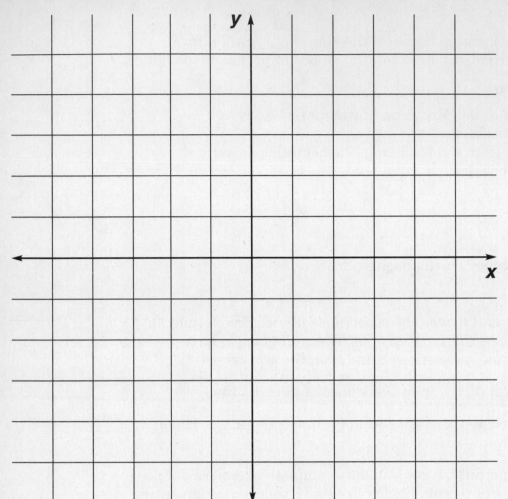

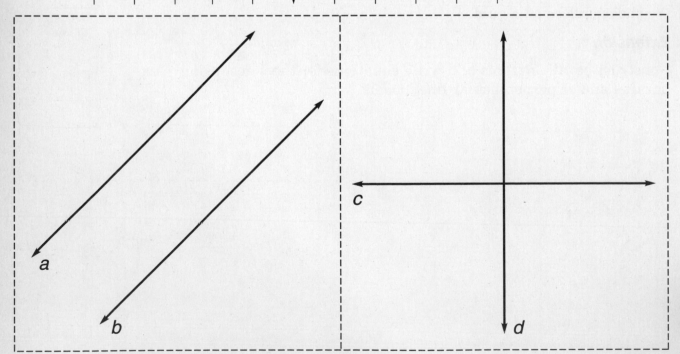

NAME_____ DATE _____

Modeling Mathematics Activity

Student Edition
Pages 362–368

Slopes of Parallel and Perpendicular Lines
Trace Figures 1 and 2 at the bottom of the sheet on tracing paper.

1. Place parallel lines a and b on the coordinate graph in five different positions. For each position, record the slope and y-intercept of lines a and b in the chart below.

2. What similarities do you find between lines a and b? _____

_____

3. Write an equation for each line using the slope-intercept form.

	Slope of line a	y-intercept of line a	Slope of line b	y-intercept of line b	Equation of line a	Equation of line b
1						
2						
3						
4						
5						

4. Place perpendicular lines c and d on the coordinate graph in five different positions. For each position, record the slope and y-intercept of lines c and d in the chart.

5. What similarities do you find between lines c and d? _____

_____

6. Write an equation for each line using the slope-intercept form.

	Slope of line c	y-intercept of line c	Slope of line d	y-intercept of line d	Equation of line c	Equation of line d
1						
2						
3						
4						
5						

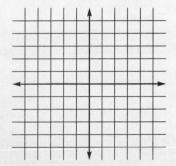

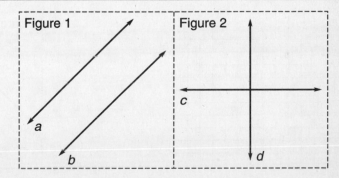

Figure 1

Figure 2

NAME_____ DATE _____

Modeling Mathematics Activity

Slopes of Parallel and Perpendicular Lines

Trace Figures 1 and 2 at the bottom of the sheet on tracing paper.

1. Place parallel lines a and b on the coordinate graph in five different positions. For each position, record the slope and y-intercept of lines a and b in the chart below. **Answers will vary.**

2. What similarities do you find between lines a and b? _____
   The slopes are the same. The *y*-intercepts are different.

3. Write an equation for each line using the slope-intercept form.
   Answers will depend upon exercise 1.

	Slope of line *a*	*y*-intercept of line *a*	Slope of line *b*	*y*-intercept of line *b*	Equation of line *a*	Equation of line *b*
1						
2						
3						
4						
5						

4. Place perpendicular lines c and d on the coordinate graph in five different positions. For each position, record the slope and y-intercept of lines c and d in the chart. **Answers will vary.**

5. What similarities do you find between lines c and d? _____
   The products of the slopes is negative one.

6. Write an equation for each line using the slope-intercept form.
   Answers will depend upon exercise 4.

	Slope of line *c*	*y*-intercept of line *c*	Slope of line *d*	*y*-intercept of line *d*	Equation of line *c*	Equation of line *d*
1						
2						
3						
4						
5						

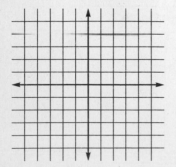

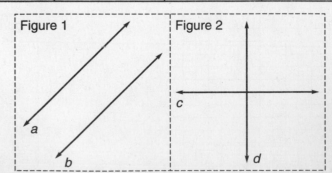

Figure 1

Figure 2

Modeling Mathematics Activity
Teaching Suggestions

Compound Inequalities

Objective

Solve compound sentences and graph the solution sets.

Materials Needed

- Classroom set of 7-4 Modeling Mathematics Activity (p. 56 in this booklet)
- Transparency from 7-4 Modeling Mathematics Activity (p. 55 in this booklet)
- Permanent HiLiter markers (1 yellow, 1 blue)

Preparation

Cut the transparencies on dotted lines and color as indicated.

Blue A ●———▶   Yellow A ●———▶
Blue B ○———▶   Yellow B ○———▶

Implementation

1. Write $x \leq 3$ on line 1 and $x > -2$ on line 2 of the transparency.

2. Graph $x \leq 3$, using the Yellow A model graph on number line 1 and model Blue B to graph $x > -2$ on line 2. (Note: Transparency can be flipped for $x < $ ____ or $x \leq $ ____ .)

3. Slide the yellow and blue models to line 3, overlapping the models. Make sure to align the origins from each graph.

4. Ask students to identify the solution sets for $x \leq 3$ *and* $x > -2$. Compare to the solution set of $x \leq 3$ *or* $x > -2$. When graphing "and" sentences, the solution set is green. Solutions to "or" sentences are yellow, blue, or green.

5. In groups or individually, use models to solve the inequalities on the worksheet.

6. Discuss the solution sets as a class.

Modeling Mathematics Activity

Compound Inequalities

1. _____

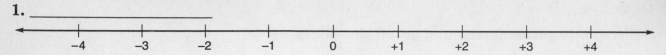

2. _____

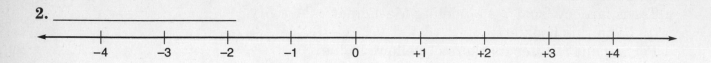

3. _____

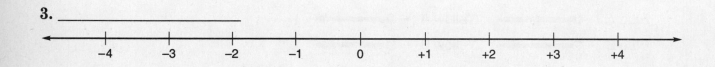

Yellow A

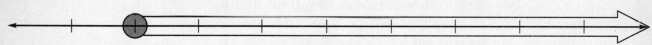

Yellow B

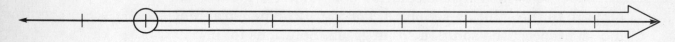

Blue A

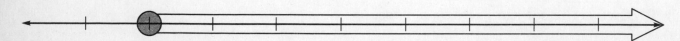

Blue B

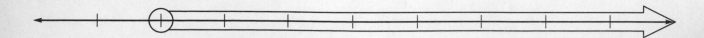

Algebra 1

7-4

Modeling Mathematics Activity

Compound Inequalities

1. Graph $x > -3$ and $x < 2$.

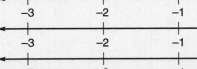

$x > -3$

$x < 2$

$-3 < x < 2$

Describe the solution set in your own words. _____

_____

2. Graph $5 > x > 0$.

$5 > x$

$x > 0$

$5 > x > 0$

Describe the solution set in your own words. _____

_____

3. Graph $x > -2$ or $x < 3$.

$x > -2$

$x < 3$

$x > -2$ or $x < 3$

Describe the solution set in your own words. _____

_____

4. Graph $x > -3$ or $x > 1$.

$x > -3$

$x > 1$

$x > -3$ or $x > 1$

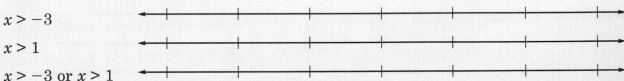

Describe the solution set in your own words. _____

_____

Modeling Mathematics Activity
Teaching Suggestions

Compound Inequalities

1. Graph $x > -3$ and $x < 2$.

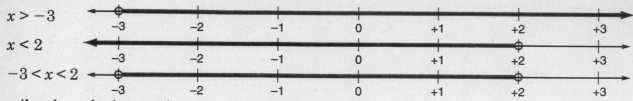

Describe the solution set in your own words. _____

All numbers between −3 and 2, but not including −3 and 2.

2. Graph $5 > x > 0$.

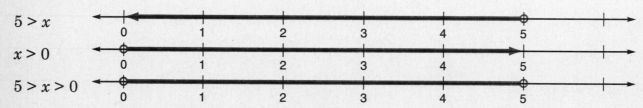

Describe the solution set in your own words. _____

All numbers between 0 and 5, but not including 0 or 5.

3. Graph $x > -2$ or $x < 3$.

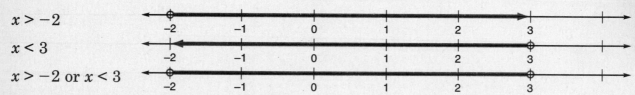

Describe the solution set in your own words. _____

All numbers between −2 and 3, but not including −2 or 3.

4. Graph $x > -3$ or $x > 1$.

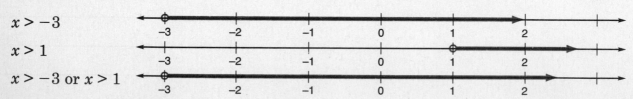

Describe the solution set in your own words. _____

All numbers greater than −3, but not including −3.

                             Algebra 1

Modeling Mathematics Activity
Teaching Suggestions

Graphing Systems of Inequalities

Objective

Solve systems of inequalities by graphing.

Materials Needed

- Classroom set of 8-5 Modeling Mathematics Activity (p. 59 in this booklet)
- Transparency from 8-5 Modeling Mathematics Activity (p. 58 in this booklet)
- Blue and yellow acetate

Preparation

Cut the transparency on the dashed lines. Cut one blue and one yellow 3" by 5" acetate rectangle per student and one set for the teacher.

Implementation

1. Review graphing linear equations and equalities. Remind students that solid lines are used for inequalities involving $\geq$ or $\leq$ and dashed lines are used for inequalities involving $>$ or $<$.

2. Graph the inequality $y > x + 2$. Place the blue acetate rectangle on the graph to illustrate the area to be shaded.

3. Next, graph $y \leq 3x$ and shade with the yellow acetate rectangle.

4. Tell students that the solution to the system $y > x + 2$ and $y \leq 3x$ is the green area on the graph.

5. In groups, have students complete the worksheet.

Modeling Mathematics Activity

Graphing Systems of Inequalities

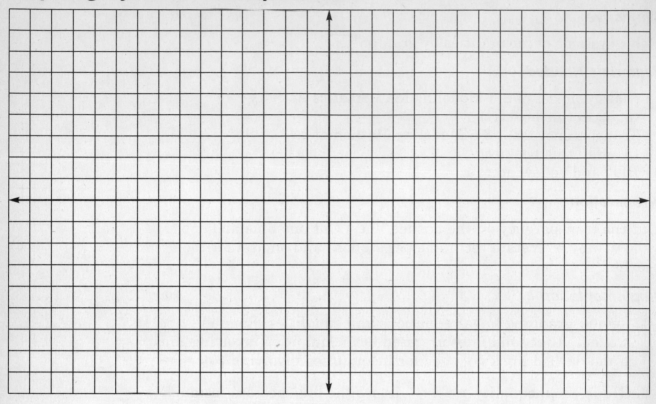

NAME_____ DATE _____

Modeling Mathematics Activity

Student Edition
Pages 482–486

Graphing Systems of Inequalities

Graph each inequality.

1. $x > 2$

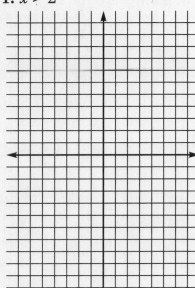

2. $y < x - 1$

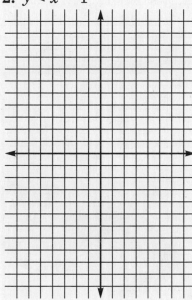

3. $2x + y \geq 6$

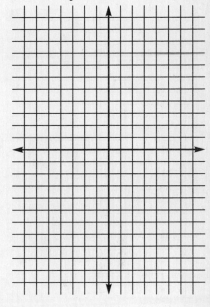

Solve each system of inequalities by graphing.

4. $y > 4$
    $x \leq -1$

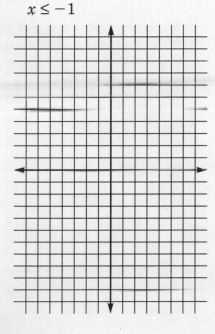

5. $y \geq x + 4$
    $y < 2x - 2$

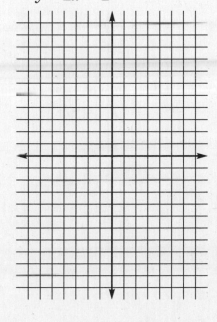

6. $x - y > 1$
    $y - x > 1$

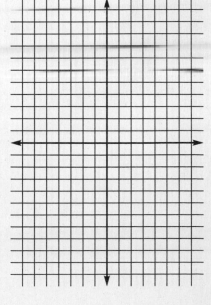

Algebra 1

NAME _____ DATE _____

Modeling Mathematics Activity

Graphing Systems of Inequalities

Graph each inequality.

1. $x > 2$

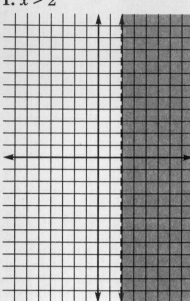

2. $y < x - 1$

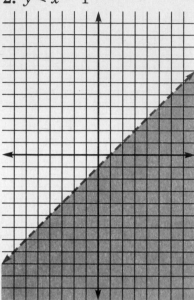

3. $2x + y \geq 6$

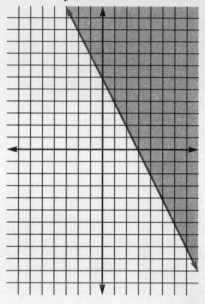

Solve each system of inequalities by graphing.

4. $y > 4$
   $x \leq -1$

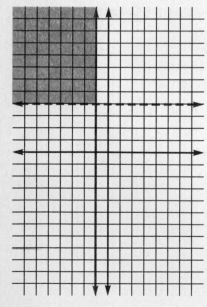

5. $y \geq x + 4$
   $y < 2x - 2$

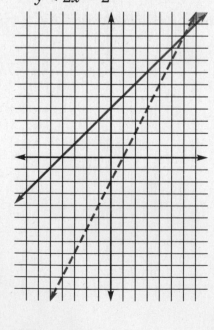

6. $x - y > 1$
   $y - x > 1$

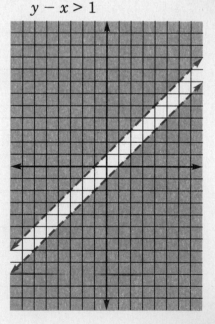

Algebra 1

Modeling Mathematics Activity
Teaching Suggestions

Multiplying Polynomials

Objective

Multiply polynomials by using the distributive property.

Materials Needed

- Classroom set of 9-7 Modeling Mathematics Activity (p. 62 in this booklet)
- Transparency from 9-7 Modeling Mathematics Activity (p. 61 in this booklet)
- Models: 3 squares (x by x)
  10 rectangles (1 by x)
  8 squares (1 by 1)

Preparation

Cut the figures on the transparency that are below the dashed line and color them if you wish. You may want to make similar sets of squares and rectangles for students from heavy paper.

Implementation

1. Discuss how to find the area of figures A–D on the transparency. Remind students that the area of a rectangle is the product of its length and width.
   A Area $= 6 \cdot 6$
   B Area $= (6 \cdot 4) + (6 \cdot 2)$ Be sure students understand
   C Area $= (6 \cdot 6) + (6 \cdot (-2))$ that this is an application
   D Area $= (3 \cdot 4) + (3 \cdot 2) + (3 \cdot 4) + (3 \cdot 2)$ of the distributive property.

2. Have students complete exercises 1–3 on the worksheet.

3. Assign areas values to models: x by $x = x^2$, 1 by $x = x$, and 1 by 1 = 1.

4. Place the models over matching spaces of figures E–H on the transparency. Discuss finding their products by adding the areas.
   E Area $= x(x + 1) = x^2 + x$
   F Area $= x(x + 3) = x^2 + 3x$
   G Area $= x(x - 2) = x^2 - 2x$
   H Area $= (x + 1)(x + 4) = x^2 + 5x + 4$

5. In groups, have students use diagrams or models to complete the worksheet.

Extension

Factor polynomials by creating a rectangle and working backwards.

Modeling Mathematics Activity

Multiplying Polynomials

Find the area of the region bounded by the solid line.

A
6
6

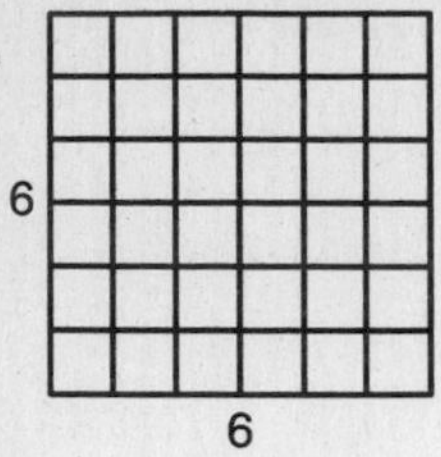

B
6
4 + 2

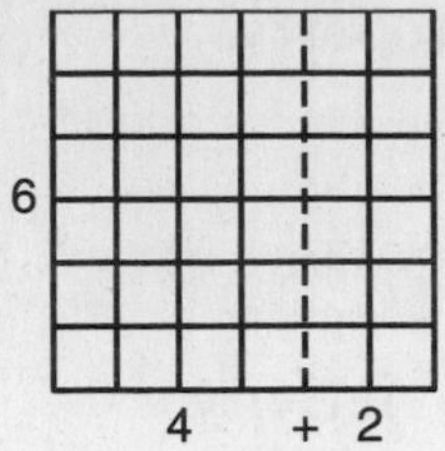

C
6
⊢ 2 ⊣
⊢ 6 ⊣

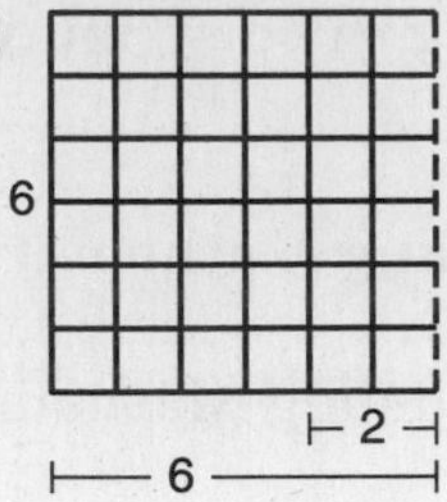

D
3
+
3
4 + 2

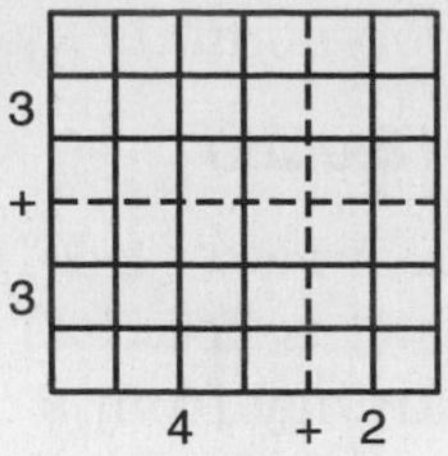

E
x
x +1

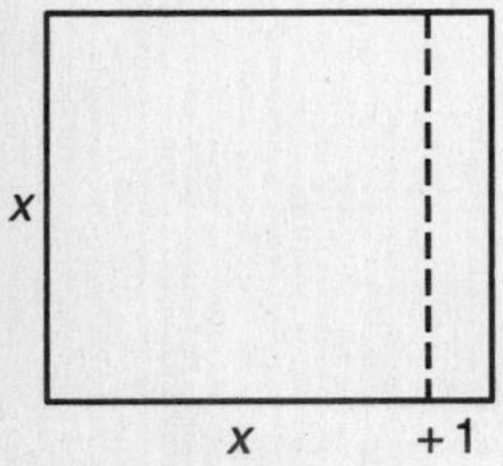

F
x
x ⊢ 3 ⊣

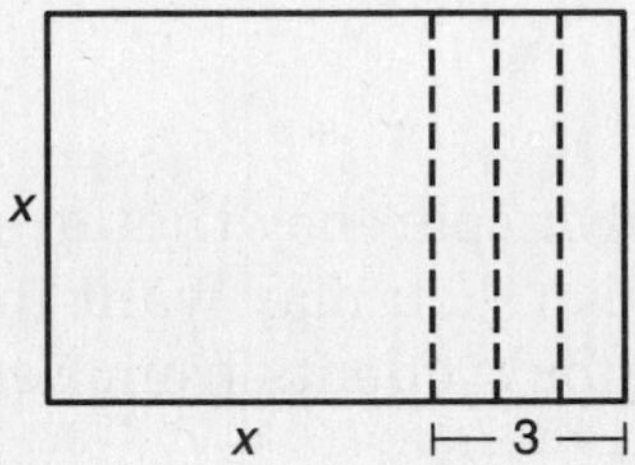

G
x
⊢ 2 ⊣
⊢ x ⊣

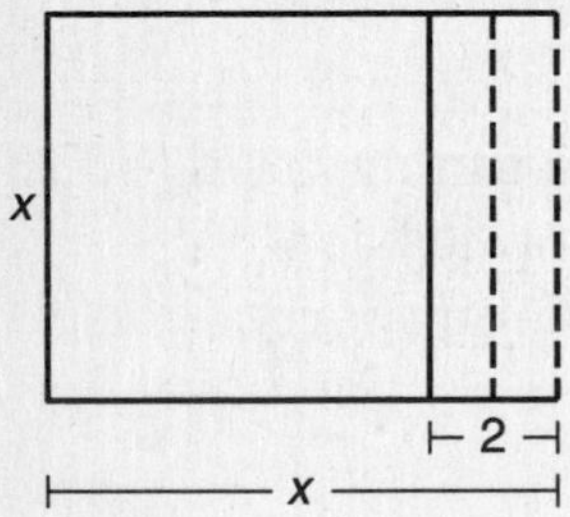

H
x
+
1
x + 4

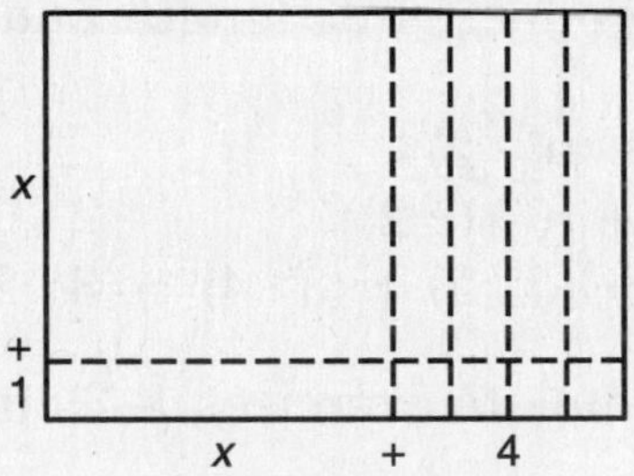

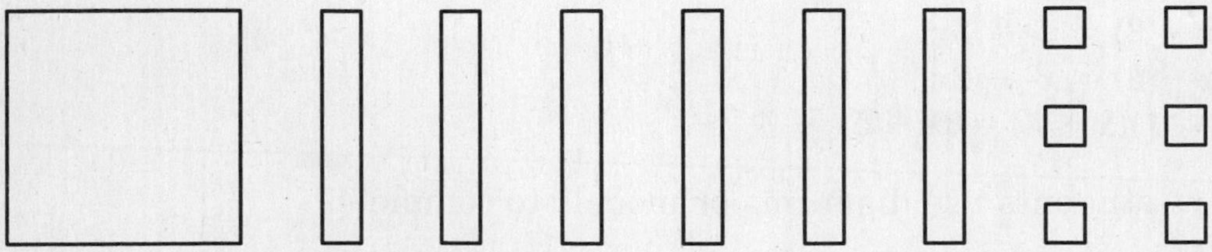

NAME_____ DATE _____

Modeling Mathematics Activity

Multiplying Polynomials

Draw a diagram and find each product.

Example: $6(3 + 3)$

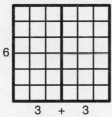

6

3 + 3

$= \underline{6 \cdot 3 + 6 \cdot 3 = 36}$

1. $6(1 + 5)$

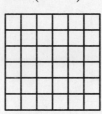

$=$ _____

2. $6(6 - 2)$

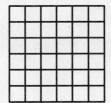

$=$ _____

3. $(4 + 2)(1 + 5)$

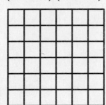

$=$ _____

Example: $x(x - 1)$

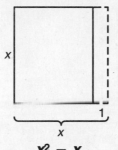

x

1

x

$= \underline{x^2 - x}$

4. $x(x - 2)$

$=$ _____

5. $x(x + 3)$

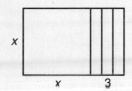

x

x   3

$=$ _____

6. $(x + 1)(x + 2)$

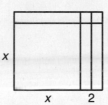

x

x   2

$=$ _____

7. $(x + 4)(x - 3)$

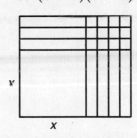

x

x

$=$ _____

Draw a diagram or use models to find each product.

8. $3(x + 1) =$ _____

9. $2(x - 8) =$ _____

10. $x(x + 3) =$ _____

11. $x(x - 4) =$ _____

12. $x(3x + 2) =$ _____

13. $(x + 2)(x + 8) =$ _____

Algebra 1

Modeling Mathematics Activity

Multiplying Polynomials

Draw a diagram and find each product.

Example: $6(3 + 3)$

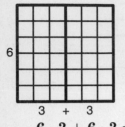

$$3 + 3$$
$$= \underline{6 \cdot 3 + 6 \cdot 3 = 36}$$

1. $6(1 + 5)$

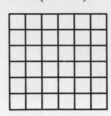

$$= \underline{(6 \cdot 1) + (6 \cdot 5) = 36}$$

2. $6(6 - 2)$

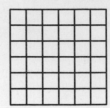

$$= \underline{(6 \cdot 6) + (6 \cdot (-2)) = 24}$$

3. $(4 + 2)(1 + 5)$

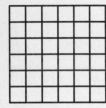

$$\underline{\begin{array}{l}(4 \cdot 1) + (4 \cdot 5) + \\ (2 \cdot 1) + (2 \cdot 5) = 36\end{array}}$$

Example: $x(x - 1)$

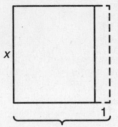

$$= \underline{x^2 - x}$$

4. $x(x - 2)$

$$\underline{\begin{array}{l}(x \cdot x) + (x \cdot (-2)) = \\ x^2 - 2x\end{array}}$$

5. $x(x + 3)$

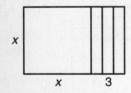

$$= \underline{x^2 + 3x}$$

6. $(x + 1)(x + 2)$

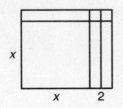

$$= \underline{x^2 + 3x + 2}$$

7. $(x + 4)(x - 3)$

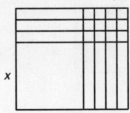

$$= \underline{x^2 + x - 12}$$

Draw a diagram or use models to find each product.

8. $3(x + 1) = \underline{\quad 3x + 3 \quad}$

9. $2(x - 8) = \underline{\quad 2x - 16 \quad}$

10. $x(x + 3) = \underline{\quad x^2 + 3x \quad}$

11. $x(x - 4) = \underline{\quad x^2 - 4x \quad}$

12. $x(3x + 2) = \underline{\quad 3x^2 + 2x \quad}$

13. $(x + 2)(x + 8) = \underline{\quad x^2 + 10x + 16 \quad}$

Algebra 1

Modeling Mathematics Activity
Teaching Suggestions

Factoring Trinomials

Objective

Factor polynomial expressions.

Materials Needed

- Classroom set of 10-3 Modeling Mathematics Activity (p. 65 in this booklet)
- Transparency from 10-3 Modeling Mathematics Activity (p. 64 in this booklet)
- Ceramic floor tiles (2" squares, 1" squares, 1" × 2" rectangles)

Preparation

Cut the transparency on the dashed line, then cut the squares and rectangles apart.

Implementation

1. Display the transparency on the overhead projector, covering Figures 1 and 2. Identify the area of the exposed figures.

2. Have students make a tile model of rectangle $x^2 + xy$.

3. Uncover Figure 1 on the transparency and discuss the length and width of the rectangle.

4. Repeat steps 2 and 3 for $x^2 + 2xy + y^2$.

5. As a group or individual activity, complete the worksheet.

6. Review the answers to the worksheet, using the transparency model tiles, on the overhead projector.

Modeling Mathematics Activity

Factoring Trinomials

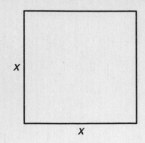

Area = _____   Area = _____   Area = _____

Figure 1   **Figure 2**

$x^2 + xy$ $x^2 + 2xy + y^2$

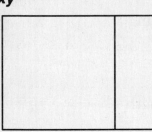   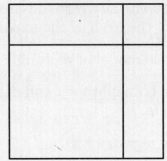

Length = _____   Length = _____

Width = _____   Width = _____

NAME_____ DATE _____

Modeling Mathematics Activity

Factoring Trinomials

$$x^2 + 5xy + 6y^2$$

1. Use ceramic floor tiles, like those shown above, to form one rectangle. Draw a picture of your rectangle below.

2. How long is your rectangle? _____ How wide is it? _____

3. What do you think the length and width of the rectangle represent?

   _____

4. Repeat the above procedure using the following polynomials and find the dimensions of the rectangles.

   a. $x^2 + 2xy + y^2$ _____

   b. $x^2 + 3xy + 2y^2$ _____

5. What conclusion can you draw regarding the dimensions of the rectangles?

   _____

   _____

   _____

Modeling Mathematics Activity

Factoring Trinomials

$$x^2 + 5xy + 6y^2$$

1. Use ceramic floor tiles, like those shown above, to form one rectangle. Draw a picture of your rectangle below.

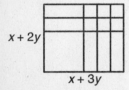

2. How long is your rectangle? __**x + 2y**__ How wide is it? __**x + 3y**__

3. What do you think the length and width of the rectangle represent?
   factors of the product of the area

4. Repeat the above procedure using the following polynomials and find the dimensions of the rectangles.

   a. $x^2 + 2xy + y^2$ **(x + y) by (x + y)**

   b. $x^2 + 3xy + 2y^2$ **(x + 2y) by (x + y)**

5. What conclusion can you draw regarding the dimensions of the rectangles?
   The dimensions of the rectangles represent the two factors of the

   trinomial, which is the area of the rectangles.

_____

Modeling Mathematics Activity
Teaching Suggestions

Factoring Trinomial Squares

Objective

Factor perfect square trinomials.

Materials Needed

- Classroom set of 10-5 Modeling Mathematics Activity (p. 68 in this booklet)

- Transparency from 10-5 Modeling Mathematics Activity (p. 67 in this booklet)

- Algebra Tiles (optional)

Preparation

Cut the transparency on the dashed line, and then cut squares and rectangles apart. Color the figures with a permanent marker if you wish.

Implementation

1. Display the transparency and identify the representation of each shape (Figure 1).

2. Arrange the models cut from the transparency to form the rectangle $x^2 + 2x + 1$ as shown below.

3. Lead a class discussion with questions such as:

   a. Is the rectangle a square? (yes)

   b. What is the length of each side of the rectangle? $(x + 1)$

   c. What is the relationship of the sides to the trinomial itself? (Point out the factors.)

4. Display each trinomial given on the transparency and arrange the models to make rectangles of each.

5. Have students cut their own models or use algebra tiles to complete the worksheet as a group or individual activity.

Modeling Mathematics Activity

Factoring Trinomial Squares

Figure 1

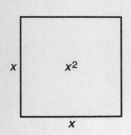 

$x^2 + 2x + 1$

$x^2 + 4x + 4$

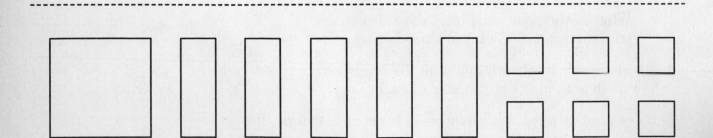

Modeling Mathematics Activity

Factoring Trinomial Squares

Use  , and $\boxed{1}$ to represent x^2, x, and 1, respectively.

Show: $x^2 + 4x + 4$ Arrange the models to form a rectangle.

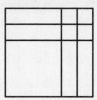

1. What do you notice about the length and width of the rectangle?

   _____

2. Give the dimensions of the final rectangle. (The dimensions are the factors of the trinomial.)

   _____

Factor by forming rectangular regions with the models.

   3. $x^2 + 6x + 9$ **4.** $4x^2 + 4x + 1$ **5.** $x^2 + 4x + 3$

   6. $x^2 + 2x + 1$ **7.** $2x^2 + 8x + 8$ **8.** $x^2 + 8x + 16$

   9. $9x^2 + 6x + 1$ **10.** $3x^2 + 4x + 1$ **11.** $x^2 - 4$

12. Which of the rectangular regions above formed squares?

   _____

13. What do you call a trinomial whose representation is a square?

   _____

14. How can you tell if a trinomial is a perfect square trinomial?

   _____

   _____

15. Describe how to factor a perfect square trinomial by inspection.

   _____

   _____

Factoring Trinomial Squares

Use  and $\boxed{1}$ to represent x^2, x, and 1, respectively.

Show: $x^2 + 4x + 4$ Arrange the models to form a rectangle.

1. What do you notice about the length and width of the rectangle?
   They're the same.

2. Give the dimensions of the final rectangle. (The dimensions are the factors of the trinomial.)
   (x + 2) by (x + 2)

Factor by forming rectangular regions with the models.

3. $x^2 + 6x + 9$
   (x + 3)(x + 3)

4. $4x^2 + 4x + 1$
   (2x + 1)(2x + 1)

5. $x^2 + 4x + 3$
   (x + 3)(x + 1)

6. $x^2 + 2x + 1$
   (x + 1)(x + 1)

7. $2x^2 + 8x + 8$
   2(x + 2)(x + 2)

8. $x^2 + 8x + 16$
   (x + 4)(x + 4)

9. $9x^2 + 6x + 1$
   (3x + 1)(3x + 1)

10. $3x^2 + 4x + 1$
    (3x + 1)(x + 1)

11. $x^2 - 4$
    (x + 2)(x - 2)

12. Which of the rectangular regions above formed squares?
    1, 3, 4, 6, 7, 8, 9 (7 forms, 2 squares)

13. What do you call a trinomial whose representation is a square?
    a perfect square trinomial

14. How can you tell if a trinomial is a perfect square trinomial?   **Quadratic term is a perfect square, constant term is a perfect square, linear term is double the product of the square roots of the other 2 terms.**

15. Describe how to factor a perfect square trinomial by inspection.
    Write 2 factors that are the sum or difference of the square root of the first and last terms (and same sign as linear term).

Modeling Mathematics Activity
Teaching Suggestions

The Pythagorean Theorem

Objective

Determine whether a triangle is a right triangle, given the lengths of its sides.

Materials Needed

- Classroom set of 13-1 Modeling Mathematics Activity (p. 71 in this booklet)
- Transparency from 13-1 Modeling Mathematics Activity (p. 70 in this booklet)
- Calculator
- Scissors
- Graph paper

Preparation

Cut the transparency on the dashed lines.

Implementation

1. Using the individual squares, demonstrate that the area of each large square equals the length of one of its sides squared.

2. Form a right triangle using sides from each square as legs.

3. In groups, have students complete exercises 1 and 2.

4. Lead a class discussion to draw conclusions about the resultant right triangle and the Pythagorean Theorem.

5. In groups, have students complete exercises 3 and 4.

6. Compile a list of the sets of squares found by students in exercise 2. Point out that if the squares of three numbers satisfy the Pythagorean Theorem, the numbers are called Pythagorean triples.

7. Have students complete exercise 5.

Extension

Discuss the length of the hypotenuse as being the distance between two points. Assist students in deriving the distance formula by using the Pythagorean Theorem.

69

The Pythagorean Theorem

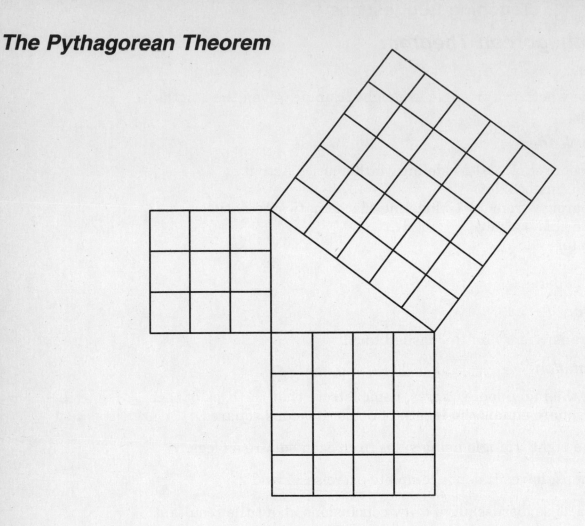

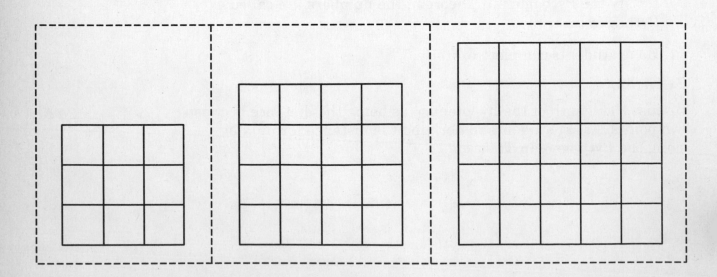

Modeling Mathematics Activity

The Pythagorean Theorem

1. Cut three squares from graph paper with sides of length 3, 4, and 5. What is the area of each square?

_____

Write an equation to show that the sum of the areas of two of the squares is equal to the area of the third square.

_____

2. Place the three squares on a sheet of paper so that their sides form a triangle. What type of triangle is it?

_____

Write an equation to show the relationship among the squares of the sides of the triangle. Let a and b represent the length of the legs and c the length of the hypotenuse.

_____

3. Find the squares of the numbers from 1 to 30. Use your calculator.

$1^2 =$ _____	$7^2 =$ _____	$13^2 =$ _____	$19^2 =$ _____	$25^2 =$ _____
$2^2 =$ _____	$8^2 =$ _____	$14^2 =$ _____	$20^2 =$ _____	$26^2 =$ _____
$3^2 =$ _____	$9^2 =$ _____	$15^2 =$ _____	$21^2 =$ _____	$27^2 =$ _____
$4^2 =$ _____	$10^2 =$ _____	$16^2 =$ _____	$22^2 =$ _____	$28^2 =$ _____
$5^2 =$ _____	$11^2 =$ _____	$17^2 =$ _____	$23^2 =$ _____	$29^2 =$ _____
$6^2 =$ _____	$12^2 =$ _____	$18^2 =$ _____	$24^2 =$ _____	$30^2 =$ _____

4. Find four sets of three squares each such that the sum of two of the squares equals the third.

_____   _____

_____   _____

5. Find the length of the hypotenuse of the right triangle given the lengths of its other sides. Use a calculator.

a. 15 feet, 36 feet _____

b. 7.5 meters, 10 meters _____

c. 8 inches, 9 inches _____

NAME_____ DATE _____

Modeling Mathematics Activity

The Pythagorean Theorem

1. Cut three squares from graph paper with sides of length 3, 4, and 5. What is the area of each square?

   9, 16, 25

   Write an equation to show that the sum of the areas of two of the squares is equal to the area of the third square.

   9 + 16 = 25 or 3² + 4² = 5²

2. Place the three squares on a sheet of paper so that their sides form a triangle. What type of triangle is it?

   right triangle

   Write an equation to show the relationship among the squares of the sides of the triangle. Let a and b represent the length of the legs and c the length of the hypotenuse.

   $a^2 + b^2 = c^2$

3. Find the squares of the numbers from 1 to 30. Use your calculator.

$1^2 =$ **1**	$7^2 =$ **49**	$13^2 =$ **169**	$19^2 =$ **361**	$25^2 =$ **625**
$2^2 =$ **4**	$8^2 =$ **64**	$14^2 =$ **196**	$20^2 =$ **400**	$26^2 =$ **676**
$3^2 =$ **9**	$9^2 =$ **81**	$15^2 =$ **225**	$21^2 =$ **441**	$27^2 =$ **729**
$4^2 =$ **16**	$10^2 =$ **100**	$16^2 =$ **256**	$22^2 =$ **484**	$28^2 =$ **784**
$5^2 =$ **25**	$11^2 =$ **121**	$17^2 =$ **289**	$23^2 =$ **529**	$29^2 =$ **841**
$6^2 =$ **36**	$12^2 =$ **144**	$18^2 =$ **324**	$24^2 =$ **576**	$30^2 =$ **900**

4. Find four sets of three squares each such that the sum of two of the squares equals the third.

   3, 4, 5; 5, 12, 13; 6, 8, 10;   **7, 24, 25; 8, 15, 17; 9, 12, 15;**

   10, 24, 26; 12, 16, 20; 15, 20, 25;   **18, 24, 30; 20, 21, 29**

5. Find the length of the hypotenuse of the right triangle given the lengths of its other sides. Use a calculator.

   a. 15 feet, 36 feet _____ **39 ft.**

   b. 7.5 meters, 10 meters _____ **12.5 m**

   c. 8 inches, 9 inches _____ **$\sqrt{145} \approx$ 12 in.**

NAME_____ DATE _____

Cooperative Learning Activity

Evaluating Expressions

Work in small groups to solve the following problems. Problem 1 is done for you.

1. Create a shape to represent the number 1. Show 3(1) and 4(2).
   Let ♥ represent 1.
   3(1) = 3 · ♥ or ♥♥♥
   4(2) = 4 · ♥♥ or ♥♥♥♥♥♥♥♥

2. Create a shape to represent x. Show $3x$, $4x$, and $2x$.

3. Show $3x$ from problem 2. Replace each x by 4. Write the value.

4. Create a shape to represent y. Show $3x$ from problem 2. Then show $3x + 2y$. Replace each x by 5 and each y by 4. Find the value.

5. Create a shape to represent x. Show $2x + 5x$. Replace x by 3. Find the value.

6. List the steps you would use to evaluate, or find the value of, an expression.

7. Use the steps you listed in problem 6 to see whether you get the correct value for each expression. (Replace each x by 5 and each y by 3.)

Expression	a. $8x + 3y$	b. $5x^2 + 2y$	c. $3x^2 + 4y^2$	d. $3(2x + y)$
Value	49	131	111	39

a.

b.

c.

d.

Cooperative Learning Activity

Evaluating Expressions

Work in small groups to solve the following problems. Problem 1 is done for you. 2–7. Sample answers are shown.

1. Create a shape to represent the number 1. Show 3(1) and 4(2).
Let ♥ represent 1.
$3(1) = 3 \cdot ♥$ or ♥♥♥
$4(2) = 4 \cdot ♥♥$ or ♥♥♥♥♥♥♥♥

2. Create a shape to represent x. Show $3x$, $4x$, and $2x$.
Let ♦ represent x.
$3x = 3 \cdot ♦$, or ♦♦♦
$4x = 4 \cdot ♦$, or ♦♦♦♦
$2x = 2 \cdot ♦$, or ♦♦

3. Show $3x$ from problem 2. Replace each x by 4. Write the value.
$3x = ♦♦♦ = 4 + 4 + 4$
$ = 12$

4. Create a shape to represent y. Show $3x$ from problem 2. Then show $3x + 2y$. Replace each x by 5 and each y by 4. Find the value.
Let ♠ represent y.
$3x + 2y = ♦♦♦ + ♠♠$
$ = 5 + 5 + 5 + 4 + 4 = 23$

5. Create a shape to represent x. Show $2x + 5x$. Replace x by 3. Find the value.
Let ♦ represent x.
$2x + 5x = ♦♦ + ♦♦♦♦♦$
$ = 2 \cdot 3 + 5 \cdot 3$
$ = 6 + 15$, or 21

6. List the steps you would use to evaluate, or find the value of, an expression.
1. **Replace each variable by the number given.**
2. **Simplify expressions inside grouping symbols.**
3. **Find the values of the powers.**
4. **Multiply and divide from left to right.**
5. **Add and subtract from left to right.**

7. Use the steps you listed in problem 6 to see whether you get the correct value for each expression. (Replace each x by 5 and each y by 3.)

Expression	a. $8x + 3y$	b. $5x^2 + 2y$	c. $3x^2 + 4y^2$	d. $3(2x + y)$
Value	49	131	111	39

a. $8x + 3y$
(1) $= 8 \cdot 5 + 3 \cdot 3$
(2)
(3)
(4) $= 40 + 9$
(5) $= 49$

b. $5x^2 + 2y$
(1) $= 5(5)^2 + 2(3)$
(2)
(3) $= 5(25) + 2(3)$
(4) $= 125 + 6$
(5) $= 131$

c. $3x^2 + 4y^2$
(1) $= 3(5)^2 + 4(3)^2$
(2)
(3) $= 3(25) + 4(9)$
(4) $= 75 + 36$
(5) $= 111$

d. $3(2x + y)$
(1) $= 3(2 \cdot 5 + 3)$
(2) $= 3(10 + 3)$
(3) $=$
(4) $= 3(13)$
(5) $= 39$

Cooperative Learning Activity

Adding and Subtracting Integers

Work in small groups to determine the rules for adding and subtracting integers. Trace and cut 10 copies of the shape at the right out of heavy paper or cardboard. Cut on the dashed line, too.

[shape] and [shape] are opposites. Their sum is zero.

Example: $-3 + 1 =$

[diagram of shapes]

$$= \boxed{-} + 0 = \boxed{-} \text{, or } -2$$

Use your models to show each sum.

1. $6 + 3$ 2. $-7 + 2$

3. $-3 + (-4)$ 4. $-5 + (-2)$

5. $1 + 4$ 6. $-3 + 7$

7. Write your rule for adding two positive integers.

8. Write your rule for adding two negative integers.

9. Write your rule for adding one positive integer and one negative integer.

Use your models to find each difference.

10. $8 - 2$ 11. $-6 - (-1)$ 12. $6 - 4$

13. $5 - 6$ (Hint: Write $5 - 6$ as $5 + (-6)$.)

14. $-2 - (-3)$ 15. $3 - (-2)$ 16. $-4 - 3$

Cooperative Learning Activity

Adding and Subtracting Integers

Work in small groups to determine the rules for adding and subtracting integers. Trace and cut 10 copies of the shape at the right out of heavy paper or cardboard. Cut on the dashed line, too.

and are opposites. Their sum is zero.

Example: $-3 + 1 =$

Use your models to show each sum.

1. $6 + 3$ **9**

2. $-7 + 2$ **−5**

3. $-3 + (-4)$ **−7**

4. $-5 + (-2)$ **−7**

5. $1 + 4$ **5**

6. $-3 + 7$ **4**

7. Write your rule for adding two positive integers. **Sample answer: Add the integers as whole numbers; the answer is a positive integer.**

8. Write your rule for adding two negative integers. **Sample answer: Ignore the negative signs and add the integers as whole numbers; the answer is a negative number.**

9. Write your rule for adding one positive integer and one negative integer. **Sample answer: Ignore the negative signs and subtract the smaller number from the larger; the answer is positive if the larger whole number is positive and negative if the larger whole number is negative.**

Use your models to find each difference.

10. $8 - 2$ **6**

11. $-6 - (-1)$ **−5**

12. $6 - 4$ **2**

13. $5 - 6$ (Hint: Write $5 - 6$ as $5 + (-6)$.)   **−1**

14. $-2 - (-3)$ **1**

15. $3 - (-2)$ **5**

16. $-4 - 3$ **−7**

NAME_____ DATE _____

Cooperative Learning Activity

Using Logic

Work in small groups. Study the following and solve the problems.

The circuits of a computer can be described using the laws of logic.

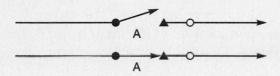

With switch A open, no current flows. The value 0 is assigned to an open switch. With switch A closed, current flows. The value 1 is assigned to a closed switch.

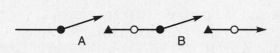

With switches A and B open, no current flows. This circuit represents the **conjunction** "A and B," which we label A ∧ B.

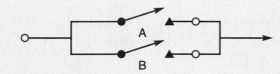

In this circuit, current flows if A or B is closed. This circuit represents the **disjunction** "A or B," which we label A ∨ B.

A	B	A ∨ B
0	0	0
0	1	1
1	0	1
1	1	1

The truth table at the left describes the truth (1) or falsity (0) of A ∨ B for all possible truth values of A and B.

In the table, 0 also represents no current flow and 1 represents current flow. Notice that the only time current does not flow through the circuit is when both switches A and B are open. Similarly, the disjunction A ∨ B is false only when statements A and B are both false.

Draw a circuit diagram for each expression.

1. (A ∧ B) ∨ C

2. (A ∨ B) ∧ C

3. (A ∨ B) ∧ (C ∨ D)

4. (A ∧ B) ∨ (C ∧ D)

5. Construct a truth table for the following circuit. There are eight rows in the table.

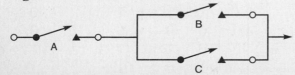

A	B	C	B ∨ C	A ∧ (B ∨ C)

Cooperative Learning Activity

Using Logic

Work in small groups. Study the following and solve the problems.

The circuits of a computer can be described using the laws of logic.

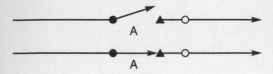

With switch A open, no current flows. The value 0 is assigned to an open switch. With switch A closed, current flows. The value 1 is assigned to a closed switch.

With switches A and B open, no current flows. This circuit represents the **conjunction** "A and B," which we label A ∧ B.

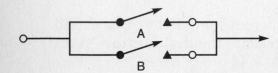

In this circuit, current flows if A or B is closed. This circuit represents the **disjunction** "A or B," which we label A ∨ B.

A	B	A ∨ B
0	0	0
0	1	1
1	0	1
1	1	1

The truth table at the left describes the truth (1) or falsity (0) of A ∨ B for all possible truth values of A and B.

In the table, 0 also represents no current flow and 1 represents current flow. Notice that the only time current does not flow through the circuit is when both switches A and B are open. Similarly, the disjunction A ∨ B is false only when statements A and B are both false.

Draw a circuit diagram for each expression.

1. (A ∧ B) ∨ C

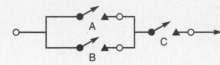

2. (A ∨ B) ∧ C

3. (A ∨ B) ∧ (C ∨ D)

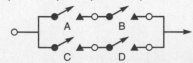

4. (A ∧ B) ∨ (C ∧ D)

5. Construct a truth table for the following circuit. There are eight rows in the table.

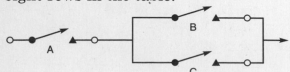

A	B	C	B ∨ C	A ∧ (B ∨ C)
0	0	0	0	0
0	0	1	1	0
0	1	0	1	0
0	1	1	1	0
1	0	0	0	0
1	0	1	1	1
1	1	0	1	1
1	1	1	1	1

Cooperative Learning Activity

The Music Business

Work in pairs to solve the problems.

Many expenses are involved in producing tapes and CDs and getting them to the consumer. For example, a record company must provide a studio, backup musicians, a producer, technicians, and recording equipment, as well as pay the artist. Then a wholesaler provides storage and transportation. A rackjobber provides tapes and CDs to a number of retailers in an area. And finally the retailer has expenses involved in sales, advertising, marketing, and so on.

Example: A tape costs $4.18 to produce. The record company uses markups to determine the cost to the consumer, as follows.

a. Record company to wholesaler, 20% markup:
$4.18 + 0.20($4.18) = $4.18 + $0.84 = $5.02

b. Wholesaler to rackjobber, 15% markup:
$5.02 + 0.15($5.02) = $5.02 + $0.75 = $5.77

c. Rackjobber to retailer, 15% markup:
$5.77 + 0.15($5.77) = $5.77 + $0.87 = $6.64

d. Retailer to consumer, 40% markup:
$6.64 + 0.40($6.64) = $6.64 + $2.66 = $9.30

The consumer must pay $9.30 for the tape.

Answer the following questions.

1. Use the markups given in the example to find the price a consumer pays for a CD that costs the record company $5.00 to produce.

2. If a CD sells at a record store for $15.98, how much did it cost the record company to produce?

3. Each time a song is played on the air, the radio station must pay $0.06 to a royalty society. Of this amount, the society keeps 15% for its expenses. Then 75% of the remainder is paid to a music publishing company and 25% is paid to the songwriter. A network of 75 stations each played "I've Got the Lonesome-For-You Blues" 4 times a day during the first 2 weeks after its release, 11 times a day during the next 2 weeks, 20 times a day for the next 3 weeks, and 8 times a day for the next 3 weeks. How much would the royalty society, the publisher, and the songwriter each receive?

Cooperative Learning Activity

The Music Business

Work in pairs to solve the problems.

Many expenses are involved in producing tapes and CDs and getting them to the consumer. For example, a record company must provide a studio, backup musicians, a producer, technicians, and recording equipment, as well as pay the artist. Then a wholesaler provides storage and transportation. A rackjobber provides tapes and CDs to a number of retailers in an area. And finally the retailer has expenses involved in sales, advertising, marketing, and so on.

Example: A tape costs $4.18 to produce. The record company uses markups to determine the cost to the consumer, as follows.

a. Record company to wholesaler, 20% markup:
$4.18 + 0.20($4.18) = $4.18 + $0.84 = $5.02

b. Wholesaler to rackjobber, 15% markup:
$5.02 + 0.15($5.02) = $5.02 + $0.75 = $5.77

c. Rackjobber to retailer, 15% markup:
$5.77 + 0.15($5.77) = $5.77 + $0.87 = $6.64

d. Retailer to consumer, 40% markup:
$6.64 + 0.40($6.64) = $6.64 + $2.66 = $9.30

The consumer must pay $9.30 for the tape.

Answer the following questions.

1. Use the markups given in the example to find the price a consumer pays for a CD that costs the record company $5.00 to produce. **$11.12**

2. If a CD sells at a record store for $15.98, how much did it cost the record company to produce? **$7.19**

3. Each time a song is played on the air, the radio station must pay $0.06 to a royalty society. Of this amount, the society keeps 15% for its expenses. Then 75% of the remainder is paid to a music publishing company and 25% is paid to the songwriter. A network of 75 stations each played "I've Got the Lonesome-For-You Blues" 4 times a day during the first 2 weeks after its release, 11 times a day during the next 2 weeks, 20 times a day for the next 3 weeks, and 8 times a day for the next 3 weeks. How much would the royalty society, the publisher, and the songwriter each receive? **$538.65; $2289.26; $763.09**

NAME_____ DATE _____

Cooperative Learning Activity

Functions or Not?

Work in pairs. Use the materials listed below to complete the activities on this page.

Materials needed: one red die
one green die
graph paper
ruler

Roll each die four times to complete the chart. Write the results as ordered pairs.

Red	Green

Plot the ordered pairs on the grid below.

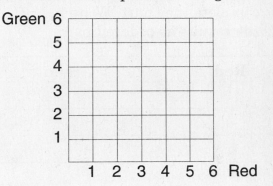

Use the information from the activity above to answer the following questions.

1. What is the relation? Write as a set of ordered pairs.

2. What is the domain of the relation?

3. What is the range?

4. The vertical line test for a function states that if any vertical line passes through no more than one point of the graph of a relation, then the relation is a function. Does the vertical line test indicate that this relation is a function?

5. Repeat the experiment three times. Answer the questions for each experiment. Can you make any generalizations about the results?

Cooperative Learning Activity

Functions or Not?

Work in pairs. Use the materials listed below to complete the activities on this page.

Materials needed: one red die
one green die
graph paper
ruler

Roll each die four times to complete the chart. Write the results as ordered pairs.

Red	Green

Plot the ordered pairs on the grid below.

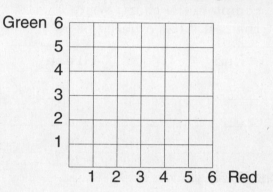

Use the information from the activity above to answer the following questions.

1. What is the relation? Write as a set of ordered pairs.
   1–4: Answers will vary.

2. What is the domain of the relation?

3. What is the range?

4. The vertical line test for a function states that if any vertical line passes through no more than one point of the graph of a relation, then the relation is a function. Does the vertical line test indicate that this relation is a function?

5. Repeat the experiment three times. Answer the questions for each experiment. Can you make any generalizations about the results?
   Students may find in individual experiments that the vertical line test indicates that the relation is a function. However, it is likely that sooner or later the relation will prove not to be a function—that is, a result on the red die will be paired with two or more results on the green die.

Olympic Women's Shot-Put Winners

Work in small groups to solve the following problems about the Olympic Games.

The Games are held every four years. The women's shot put was introduced as an Olympic event in 1948. Listed below are the gold medalists and their winning distances.

Year	Winner	Distance (in meters)
1948	Ostermeyer (France)	13.75
1952	Zybina (U.S.S.R.)	15.28
1956	Tishkyevich (U.S.S.R.)	16.59
1960	Press (U.S.S.R.)	17.32
1964	Press (U.S.S.R.)	18.14
1968	Gummel (East Germany)	19.61
1972	Chizhova (U.S.S.R.)	21.03
1976	Christova (Bulgaria)	21.16
1980	Sluplanek (East Germany)	22.41

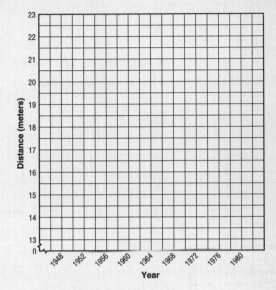

Do these problems.

1. Plot the data given above in the coordinate plane provided.

2. Draw a single straight line that you think best represents the data. The number of points above your line should be about the same as the number of points below the line. This line is called the "line of best fit."

3. Use two points from your line of best fit to find the equation of the line.

Use the equation you found in problem 3 to answer problems 4–6.

4. Predict the winning distance in the year 2000.

5. Predict when the winning distance will first be more than 30 meters.

6. Predict what the winning distance would have been had the women's shot put been an event in the 1908 Olympics.

7. The winner of the women's shot put in 1984 was Losch (W. Germany). Her distance was 20.48 meters. Do some research to find why the winning distance might have been so short in 1984.

Cooperative Learning Activity

Olympic Women's Shot-Put Winners

Work in small groups to solve the following problems about the Olympic Games.

The Games are held every four years. The women's shot put was introduced as an Olympic event in 1948. Listed below are the gold medalists and their winning distances.

Year	Winner	Distance (in meters)
1948	Ostermeyer (France)	13.75
1952	Zybina (U.S.S.R.)	15.28
1956	Tishkyevich (U.S.S.R.)	16.59
1960	Press (U.S.S.R.)	17.32
1964	Press (U.S.S.R.)	18.14
1968	Gummel (East Germany)	19.61
1972	Chizhova (U.S.S.R.)	21.03
1976	Christova (Bulgaria)	21.16
1980	Sluplanek (East Germany)	22.41

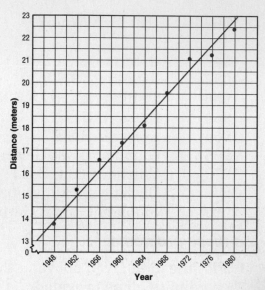

Do these problems.

1. Plot the data given above in the coordinate plane provided.
   See students' graphs.

2. Draw a single straight line that you think best represents the data. The number of points above your line should be about the same as the number of points below the line. This line is called the "line of best fit."
   A possible answer is shown; see students' graphs.

3. Use two points from your line of best fit to find the equation of the line. **Possible answer: $2x - 7y = 3800$**

Use the equation you found in problem 3 to answer problems 4–6.

4. Predict the winning distance in the year 2000.
   Possible prediction: 28.57 m

5. Predict when the winning distance will first be more than 30 meters.
   Possible prediction: 2008

6. Predict what the winning distance would have been had the women's shot put been an event in the 1908 Olympics.
   Possible prediction: 2.29 m

7. The winner of the women's shot put in 1984 was Losch (W. Germany). Her distance was 20.48 meters. Do some research to find why the winning distance might have been so short in 1984. **The Soviet Union and its allies boycotted the Olympics in 1984. In view of the dominance of the event by this group in previous Olympics, the best athletes did not compete in 1984.**

Multiplying Inequalities by −1

Work with a partner. Be sure that each of you understands each step in the examples.

Example 1: Solve the inequality.

$$3 - x < -2x$$
$$3 - x + 2x < -2x + 2x \qquad \textit{Add 2x to each side.}$$
$$3 + x < 0$$
$$3 + x - 3 < 0 - 3 \qquad \textit{Subtract 3 from each side.}$$
$$x < -3$$

Example 2: Suppose that the inequality symbol is an equality symbol in Example 1. The equation might be solved as follows.

$$3 - x = -2x$$
$$3 - x + x = -2x + x \qquad \textit{Add x to each side.}$$
$$3 = -x$$
$$-3 = x \qquad \textit{Multiply each side by −1.}$$

Example 3: Try to solve the inequality as the equation was solved.

$$3 - x < -2x$$
$$3 - x + x < -2x + x \qquad \textit{Add x to each side.}$$
$$3 < -x$$

Another way to state the inequality $3 < -x$ is $-x > 3$. Recall that the solution in Example 1 is $x < -3$. The inequalities $-x > 3$ and $x < -3$ are equivalent. Notice that the directions of the inequality symbols are reversed. In the last step of Example 2, each side of the equation is multiplied by −1. Finish the solution of the inequality.

$$3 < -x$$
$$-3 > x \qquad \textit{Multiply each side by −1.}$$

State the rule for multiplying an inequality by − 1.

Multiply each side of the following inequalities by − 1.

1. $-x > 2$
2. $-x < 5$
3. $x < 6$
4. $x > -7$

5. $-x < -4$
6. $-x > -8$
7. $x < -10$
8. $-x > 0$

9. Complete the following.
   If $a < b$, then $(-1)(a)$ _____ $(-1)(b)$.

   If $a > b$, then $(-1)(a)$ _____ $(-1)(b)$.

10. What do you suppose is the result of multiplying each side of an inequality by any negative number?

NAME_____ DATE _____

Cooperative Learning Activity

Student Edition
Pages 384–390

Multiplying Inequalities by −1

Work with a partner. Be sure that each of you understands each step in the examples.

Example 1: Solve the inequality.

$$3 - x < -2x$$
$$3 - x + 2x < -2x + 2x \qquad \text{Add } 2x \text{ to each side.}$$
$$3 + x < 0$$
$$3 + x - 3 < 0 - 3 \qquad \text{Subtract 3 from each side.}$$
$$x < -3$$

Example 2: Suppose that the inequality symbol is an equality symbol in Example 1. The equation might be solved as follows.

$$3 - x = -2x$$
$$3 - x + x = -2x + x \qquad \text{Add } x \text{ to each side.}$$
$$3 = -x$$
$$-3 = x \qquad \text{Multiply each side by } -1.$$

Example 3: Try to solve the inequality as the equation was solved.

$$3 - x < -2x$$
$$3 - x + x < -2x + x \qquad \text{Add } x \text{ to each side.}$$
$$3 < -x$$

Another way to state the inequality $3 < -x$ is $-x > 3$. Recall that the solution in Example 1 is $x < -3$. The inequalities $-x > 3$ and $x < -3$ are equivalent. Notice that the directions of the inequality symbols are reversed. In the last step of Example 2, each side of the equation is multiplied by -1. Finish the solution of the inequality.

$$3 < -x$$
$$-3 > x \qquad \text{Multiply each side by } -1.$$

State the rule for multiplying an inequality by -1.

Multiply each side of the following inequalities by − 1.

1. $-x > 2$
   $x < -2$
2. $-x < 5$
   $x > -5$
3. $x < 6$
   $-x > -6$
4. $x > -7$
   $-x < 7$

5. $-x < -4$
   $x > 4$
6. $-x > -8$
   $x < 8$
7. $x < -10$
   $-x > 10$
8. $-x > 0$
   $x < 0$

9. Complete the following.

   If $a < b$, then $(-1)(a)$ __**>**__ $(-1)(b)$.

   If $a > b$, then $(-1)(a)$ __**<**__ $(-1)(b)$.

10. What do you suppose is the result of multiplying each side of an inequality by any negative number? **The direction of the inequality symbol must be reversed.**

 Algebra 1

NAME _____ DATE _____

Cooperative Learning Activity

Comparing Options

Work in pairs. Suppose there will be five 100-point tests each quarter in algebra class. Homework will be checked 25 times each quarter. You figure that you can average 70 points on each of the 5 tests for a total of 70(5), or 350, points.

You are given two options for calculating your grade. The first option is to have 5 points taken off the total of your test scores each time you fail to do a homework assignment.

The second option is to have 4 points added to your total each time you do an assignment. The second option results in the homework acting as a sixth test worth 4(25), or 100, points.

The ratio $y = \dfrac{\text{(your points)}}{\text{(total possible points)}}$ determines your grade. The greater the ratio, the better your grade. The highest possible grade is 1.00. Let $x =$ the number of times each quarter that you figure you will not do your homework assignment.

First option

$$y = \frac{350 - 5x}{500}$$

$$y = -\frac{5}{500}x + \frac{350}{500}$$

$$y = -\frac{1}{100}x + \frac{7}{10}$$

Second option

$$y = \frac{350 + 4(25 - x)}{600}$$

$$y = \frac{350 + 100 - 4x}{600}$$

$$y = -\frac{4}{600}x + \frac{450}{600}$$

$$y = -\frac{1}{150}x + \frac{3}{4}$$

1. Use the coordinate plane provided at the right to graph both equations on one coordinate system. Which option will give you a higher grade? Remember, the greater the value of y, the better the grade.

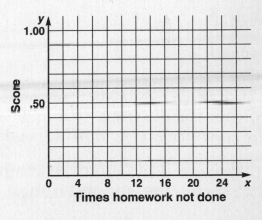

2. Suppose you figure that you can average 80 rather than 70 on the 5 tests. Use the example above to help you derive an equation for each option. Graph each equation on the second coordinate plane. Which option will give you a higher grade?

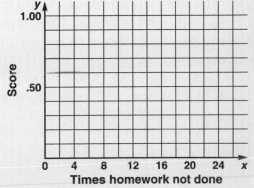

Cooperative Learning Activity

Comparing Options

Work in pairs. Suppose there will be five 100-point tests each quarter in algebra class. Homework will be checked 25 times each quarter. You figure that you can average 70 points on each of the 5 tests for a total of 70(5), or 350, points.

You are given two options for calculating your grade. The first option is to have 5 points taken off the total of your test scores each time you fail to do a homework assignment.

The second option is to have 4 points added to your total each time you do an assignment. The second option results in the homework acting as a sixth test worth 4(25), or 100, points.

The ratio $y = \dfrac{\text{(your points)}}{\text{(total possible points)}}$ determines your grade. The greater the ratio, the better your grade. The highest possible grade is 1.00. Let $x =$ the number of times each quarter that you figure you will not do your homework assignment.

First option

$$y = \frac{350 - 5x}{500}$$

$$y = -\frac{5}{500}x + \frac{350}{500}$$

$$y = -\frac{1}{100}x + \frac{7}{10}$$

Second option

$$y = \frac{350 + 4(25 - x)}{600}$$

$$y = \frac{350 + 100 - 4x}{600}$$

$$y = -\frac{4}{600}x + \frac{450}{600}$$

$$y = -\frac{1}{150}x + \frac{3}{4}$$

1. Use the coordinate plane provided at the right to graph both equations on one coordinate system. Which option will give you a higher grade? Remember, the greater the value of y, the better the grade. **the second option**

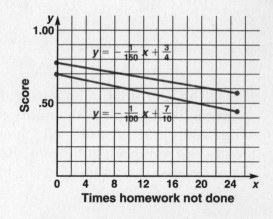

2. Suppose you figure that you can average 80 rather than 70 on the 5 tests. Use the example above to help you derive an equation for each option. Graph each equation on the second coordinate plane. Which option will give you a higher grade? **the second option**

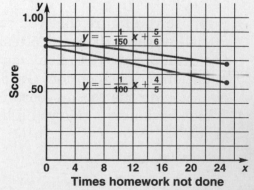

Cooperative Learning Activity

Multiplying Binomials

Work in small groups. You can find the product of two binomials, $(x + 1)(3x - 2)$, by finding the area of a rectangle.

Step 1 Draw a rectangle whose width represents one binomial and whose length represents the other binomial. Use a longer segment to represent x and a shorter segment to represent 1. $-x$ and -1 can be represented by squiggly lines.

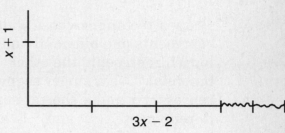

Step 2 Complete the rectangle by drawing the remaining sides of each individual rectangle. Write the area of each rectangle inside it.

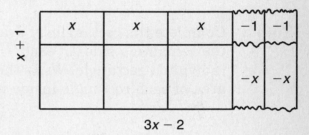

Step 3 Add the areas of the individual rectangles, combining those that are like terms.

$$\text{Area} = 3x^2 + 3x - 2x - 2$$
$$= 3x^2 + x - 2$$

Would the square at the right represent 1 or -1? Justify your answer.

Use the procedure shown above to find each product.

1. $(x + 2)(x - 3)$

2. $(x - 1)(2x + 1)$

3. $(2x - 1)(2x + 3)$

4. $(x + 3)(x - 3)$

5. $(x + 4)(x + 4)$

6. $(x - 2)(x - 2)$

NAME_____ DATE _____

Cooperative Learning Activity

Multiplying Binomials

Work in small groups. You can find the product of two binomials, $(x + 1)(3x - 2)$, by finding the area of a rectangle.

Step 1 Draw a rectangle whose width represents one binomial and whose length represents the other binomial. Use a longer segment to represent x and a shorter segment to represent 1. $-x$ and -1 can be represented by squiggly lines.

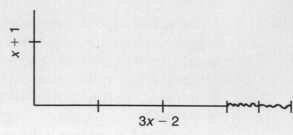

Step 2 Complete the rectangle by drawing the remaining sides of each individual rectangle. Write the area of each rectangle inside it.

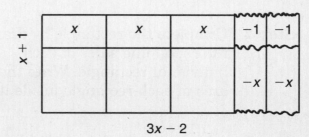

Step 3 Add the areas of the individual rectangles, combining those that are like terms.

$$\text{Area} = 3x^2 + 3x - 2x - 2$$
$$= 3x^2 + x - 2$$

Would the square at the right represent 1 or -1? Justify your answer.

Since $-1 \cdot (-1) = 1$, the square represents 1.

Use the procedure shown above to find each product.

1. $(x + 2)(x - 3)$
   $x^2 - x - 6$

2. $(x - 1)(2x + 1)$
   $2x^2 - x - 1$

3. $(2x - 1)(2x + 3)$
   $4x^2 + 4x - 3$

4. $(x + 3)(x - 3)$
   $x^2 - 9$

5. $(x + 4)(x + 4)$
   $x^2 + 8x + 16$

6. $(x - 2)(x - 2)$
   $x^2 - 4x + 4$

Factoring Trinomial Squares

Work in small groups.

Use  , and 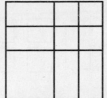 to represent x^2, x, and 1, respectively.

Use the models to represent the trinomial $x^2 + 4x + 4$.

Arrange the models to form a rectangle.

1. What do you notice about the length and width of the final rectangle?

2. Give the dimensions of the final rectangle. (The dimensions are the factors of the trinomial.)

Factor each of the following polynomials by forming rectangular regions with the models.

3. $x^2 + 6x + 9$

4. $4x^2 + 4x + 1$

5. $x^2 + 4x + 3$

6. $x^2 + 2x + 1$

7. $x^2 + 8x + 16$

8. $3x^2 + 4x + 1$

9. Which of the rectangles above are squares?

10. What do you call a trinomial whose representation is a square?

11. How can you tell whether a trinomial is a perfect square trinomial?

12. Factor $x^2 - 4$ by forming a rectangular region from two trapezoids.

Factoring Trinomial Squares

Work in small groups.

Use 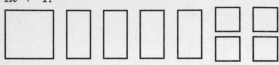 **, and** 1 **to represent** x^2**,** x**, and 1, respectively.**

Use the models to represent the trinomial $x^2 + 4x + 4$.

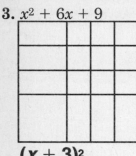

Arrange the models to form a rectangle.

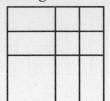

1. What do you notice about the length and width of the final rectangle?
   They are the same.

2. Give the dimensions of the final rectangle. (The dimensions are the factors of the trinomial.)
   (x + 2) by (x + 2)

Factor each of the following polynomials by forming rectangular regions with the models.

3. $x^2 + 6x + 9$

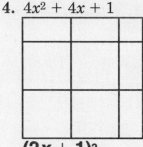

$(x + 3)^2$

4. $4x^2 + 4x + 1$

$(2x + 1)^2$

5. $x^2 + 4x + 3$

$(x + 3)(x + 1)$

6. $x^2 + 2x + 1$

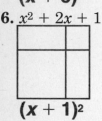

$(x + 1)^2$

7. $x^2 + 8x + 16$

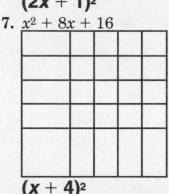

$(x + 4)^2$

8. $3x^2 + 4x + 1$

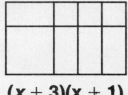

$(3x + 1)(x + 1)$

9. Which of the rectangles above are squares? $x^2 + 6x + 9$, $4x^2 + 4x + 1$, $x^2 + 2x + 1$, $x^2 + 8x + 16$

10. What do you call a trinomial whose representation is a square?
    perfect square trinomial

11. How can you tell whether a trinomial is a perfect square trinomial?
    The first and third terms are squares and the middle term is twice the product of the square roots of the first and third terms.

12. Factor $x^2 - 4$ by forming a rectangular region from two trapezoids.

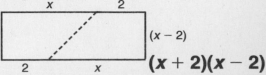

$(x + 2)(x - 2)$

Cooperative Learning Activity

Student Edition
Pages 611–617

Graphing Quadratic Functions

Work with a partner to solve the following problems.

A ball is thrown vertically into the air with a velocity of 112 feet per second. The ball was released 6 feet above the ground. The height above the ground t seconds after release is given by the formula $h = -16t^2 + 112t + 6$.

1. Complete the table using whole-number values for t.

t	h

2. Use the values in the table to graph the equation representing the height of the ball.

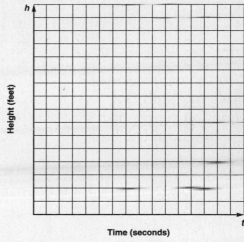

Height (feet)

Time (seconds)

3. What is the maximum height the ball achieves? Explain how you know.

4. How long did it take the ball to return to the ground?

Cooperative Learning Activity

Graphing Quadratic Functions

Work with a partner to solve the following problems.

A ball is thrown vertically into the air with a velocity of 112 feet per second. The ball was released 6 feet above the ground. The height above the ground t seconds after release is given by the formula $h = -16t^2 + 112t + 6$.

1. Complete the table using whole-number values for t.
   Sample values are shown.

t	h
0	6
1	102
2	166
3	198
3.5	202
4	198
5	166
6	102
7	6

2. Use the values in the table to graph the equation representing the height of the ball.

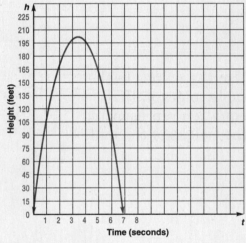

3. What is the maximum height the ball achieves? Explain how you know.
   The maximum height is 202 ft. The maximum height is at the vertex of the graph, which is at (3.5, 202).

4. How long did it take the ball to return to the ground?
   slightly longer than 7 seconds

Cooperative Learning Activity

Student Edition
Pages 696–702

Rational Roundup

Work in pairs.

Cut out the rectangles of problems. Solve the problems and match each rectangle with another one with the same answer.

A. Simplify. $\dfrac{3-c}{c-3} \div \dfrac{9-3c}{3c-9}$	**G.** Solve. $\dfrac{x-1}{x-2} = \dfrac{3}{2}$
B. Solve. $\dfrac{2}{5-x} = \dfrac{2}{x-3}$	**H.** Solve. $\dfrac{3}{2y} - \dfrac{6}{2y+y^2} = \dfrac{1}{y+2}$
C. Simplify. $\dfrac{3y+15}{y} \div \dfrac{y+5}{y}$	**I.** Simplify. $\dfrac{x-5y}{x+y} + \dfrac{x+7y}{x+y}$
D. Solve. $\dfrac{5n}{12} - \dfrac{1}{6} = \dfrac{2}{3}$	**J.** Simplify. $\dfrac{x^2+2x-15}{x^2+4x-5} \cdot \dfrac{x^2+x-2}{x^2-6-x}$
E. Simplify. $\dfrac{4x^2}{3y} \cdot \dfrac{135xy}{36x^3}$	**K.** Simplify. $\dfrac{5x-10}{3} \div \dfrac{2x-4}{6}$
F. Simplify. $\dfrac{3x+6}{5} \div \dfrac{x+2}{10}$	**L.** Simplify. $\dfrac{12x^2-48}{4x^2-16}$

Now that you have completed the match, you will see that the final answers have a mathematical relationship. What is it?

Cooperative Learning Activity

Rational Roundup

Work in pairs.

Cut out the rectangles of problems. Solve the problems and match each rectangle with another one with the same answer.

A. Simplify. $\dfrac{3-c}{c-3} \div \dfrac{9-3c}{3c-9}$ **1**	**G.** Solve. $\dfrac{x-1}{x-2} = \dfrac{3}{2}$ **4**
B. Solve. $\dfrac{2}{5-x} = \dfrac{2}{x-3}$ **4**	**H.** Solve. $\dfrac{3}{2y} - \dfrac{6}{2y+y^2} = \dfrac{1}{y+2}$ **6**
C. Simplify. $\dfrac{3y+15}{y} \div \dfrac{y+5}{y}$ **3**	**I.** Simplify. $\dfrac{x-5y}{x+y} + \dfrac{x+7y}{x+y}$ **2**
D. Solve. $\dfrac{5n}{12} - \dfrac{1}{6} = \dfrac{2}{3}$ **2**	**J.** Simplify. $\dfrac{x^2+2x-15}{x^2+4x-5} \cdot \dfrac{x^2+x-2}{x^2-6-x}$ **1**
E. Simplify. $\dfrac{4x^2}{3y} \cdot \dfrac{135xy}{36x^3}$ **5**	**K.** Simplify. $\dfrac{5x-10}{3} \div \dfrac{2x-4}{6}$ **5**
F. Simplify. $\dfrac{3x+6}{5} \div \dfrac{x+2}{10}$ **6**	**L.** Simplify. $\dfrac{12x^2-48}{4x^2-16}$ **3**

Match A and J; B and G; C and L; D and I; E and K; F and H.

Now that you have completed the match, you will see that the final answers have a mathematical relationship. What is it?

They are the first six natural numbers.

Cooperative Learning Activity

Matching Radicals

Work in pairs. Cut out the rectangles drawn below. Simplify each radical expression that can be simplified, and match it to another equivalent expression. If you do this correctly, each rectangle will match one and only one rectangle.

A	**B**	**C**	**D**
$(5 + \sqrt{2})(5 - \sqrt{2})$	$9\sqrt{3}$	$\sqrt{3}(\sqrt{6} + 2\sqrt{21})$	$20\sqrt{6}$
			$2\sqrt{30}$
$\sqrt{45} + \sqrt{80}$	62	$\sqrt{529}$	$2\sqrt{22}$

E	**F**	**G**	**H**
$5\sqrt{3} \cdot \sqrt{32}$	$\sqrt{169}$	$7\sqrt{5}$	$\sqrt{81a^2b^4}$
$\sqrt{12} \cdot \sqrt{10}$	$5\sqrt{3} + \sqrt{27} - \sqrt{48}$	$10\sqrt{30}$	$\sqrt{99}$
$\sqrt{88}$	$\sqrt{100a^4b^3}$	$8\sqrt{3} - 2\sqrt{15}$	$16\sqrt{45} - 3\sqrt{20}$

I	**J**	**K**	**L**
$3\sqrt{2} + 6\sqrt{7}$	23	$10a^2b^2$	$\sqrt{243}$
23	$7\sqrt{5}$	$3|a|b^2 \sqrt{7}$	$(8 + \sqrt{2})(8 - \sqrt{2})$

M	**N**	**O**	**P**
$\sqrt{100a^4b^4}$	13	$9|a|b^2$	$\sqrt{245}$
	$4\sqrt{3}$	$3\sqrt{11}$	$\sqrt{3000}$
$\sqrt{63a^2b^4}$	$10a^2|b|\sqrt{b}$	$42\sqrt{5}$	$\sqrt{6}(4\sqrt{2} - \sqrt{10})$

Cooperative Learning Activity

Matching Radicals

Work in pairs. Cut out the rectangles drawn below. Simplify each radical expression that can be simplified, and match it to another equivalent expression. If you do this correctly, each rectangle will match one and only one rectangle.

A J	B L	C I	D E
$(5 + \sqrt{2})(5 - \sqrt{2})$	$9\sqrt{3}$	$\sqrt{3}(\sqrt{6} + 2\sqrt{21})$	$20\sqrt{6}$
			$2\sqrt{30}$
$\sqrt{45} + \sqrt{80}$	62	$\sqrt{529}$	$2\sqrt{22}$
E **D**	**F** **N**	**G** **P**	**H** **O**
$5\sqrt{3} \cdot \sqrt{32}$	$\sqrt{169}$	$7\sqrt{5}$	$\sqrt{81a^2b^4}$
$\sqrt{12} \cdot \sqrt{10}$	$5\sqrt{3} + \sqrt{27} - \sqrt{48}$	$10\sqrt{30}$	$\sqrt{99}$
$\sqrt{88}$	$\sqrt{100a^4b^3}$	$8\sqrt{3} - 2\sqrt{15}$	$16\sqrt{45} - 3\sqrt{20}$
I **C**	**J** **A**	**K** **M**	**L** **B**
$3\sqrt{2} + 6\sqrt{7}$	23	$10a^2b^2$	$\sqrt{243}$
23	$7\sqrt{5}$	$3\lvert a \rvert b^2 \sqrt{7}$	$(8 + \sqrt{2})(8 - \sqrt{2})$
M **K**	**N** **F**	**O** **H**	**P** **G**
$\sqrt{100a^4b^4}$	13	$9\lvert a \rvert b^2$	$\sqrt{245}$
	$4\sqrt{3}$	$3\sqrt{11}$	$\sqrt{3000}$
$\sqrt{63a^2b^4}$	$10a^2\lvert b \rvert \sqrt{b}$	$42\sqrt{5}$	$\sqrt{6}(4\sqrt{2} - \sqrt{10})$

Algebra 1